Weapons of the Modern Marines

MICHAEL GREEN
AND GREG STEWART

MBI

First published in 2004 by MBI, an imprint of
MBI Publishing Company, Galtier Plaza, Suite 200,
380 Jackson Street, St. Paul, MN 55101-3885 USA

The information in this book is true and complete to
the best of our knowledge. All recommendations are
made without any guarantee on the part of the author or
Publisher, who also disclaim any liability incurred in
connection with the use of this data or specific details.

We recognize that some words, model names and designations, for example, mentioned herein are the property
of the trademark holder. We use them for identification
purposes only. This is not an official publication.

MBI titles are also available at discounts in bulk quantity
for industrial or sales-promotional use. For details write
to Special Sales Manager at Motorbooks International
Wholesalers & Distributors, Galtier Plaza, Suite 200,
380 Jackson Street, St. Paul, MN 55101-3885 USA.

Library of Congress Cataloging-in-Publication Data

Green, Michael
    Weapons of the Modern Marines / by Michael Green.
        p. cm. — (BattleGear)
    ISBN 0-7603-1697-X (alk. paper)
        1. United States. Marine Corps—Weapons Systems.
    I. Title. II. Series.

VE23.G76 2003
359.9'68'0973—dc22

On the front cover: Force Recon Marine, wearing full
spectrum battle equipment (FSBE) including body armor
and amphibious assault vest (AAV), armed with M4A1
Carbine. (Fred Pushies)

On the frontispiece: A marine is pictured ready to fire his
shoulder-launched, Redeye antiaircraft guided missile.
The missile itself came sealed inside a disposable launch
tube. It did not have a proximity warhead, as do larger
antiaircraft missiles. Instead, the onboard guidance
system would continue to make course corrections until
the last second to ensure that the missile hits its intended
target. When the missile does strike an aircraft, an
electrical pulse explodes the warhead. (Defense Visual
Information Center)

On the title page: Pictured on a firing range are marines
using an M2 .50 caliber machine gun with sandbags
on top of the tripod legs steady the gun when firing. All
machine gunners are taught that while they may not see
enemy soldiers on many occasions, they will be directed
to fire upon areas where enemy troops are suspected
to be operating. This type of firing can be extremely
effective in denying enemy units, and offers the opportunity to mass troops for an attack. (Defense Visual
Information Center)

On the back cover: Two young marines are pictured
manning an M240G 7.62mm machine gun during a training
exercise. Instead of mounting the weapon directly onto
the tripod, the connection passes through a spring-
buffered assembly on top of the tripod mount. This buffer
arrangement greatly reduces the recoil shock that the
gunner endures when firing the weapon. This in turn
allows the gunner to more closely grip his weapon when
firing and improves long-range accuracy. (Michael
Green) **Inset:** A marine takes aim with his Predator short-
range assault weapon (SRAW) at a training site. Because
the weapon arms itself only 20 yards after it leaves its
launcher, it's perfect for extremely close-range ambushes
of enemy armored fighting vehicles in towns, cities,
wooded areas, etc., that channel vehicles into areas
where they cannot move about freely or use the full
potential of their onboard weapons. (U.S. Marine Corps)

Edited by Heather Oakley and Steve Gansen
Designed by Rochelle Schultz

Printed in China

Contents

ACKNOWLEDGMENTS ACKNOWLEDGMENTS ACKNOWLEDGMENTS ACKNOWLEDGMENTS ACKNOWLEDGMENTS ACKNOWLEDGMENTS

DEDICATION

To the marines of Operation Iraqi Freedom, upholding the proud traditions of the corps.

Acknowledgments

Special thanks go to the Marine Corps public affairs men and women whose support and help made this book possible. Thanks also go to Peter Keating, director of communications at General Dynamics Land Systems Division; Herb Muktarian, manager of communications at United Defense Ground Systems Division; and Frank Hoerster, director, Fire Support Systems at BAE Systems DO for pictures and information on their various products. Jim Flynn, marketing and sales manager for General Motors Defense, also supplied pictures and background information for this book. Nettie R. Johnson, Melissa Hilliard, Peter B. Spivy, and Doug Terrell of the Lockheed Martin Missile and Fire Control also offered their assistance with pictures and information on their products.

Our good friend and fellow author Hans Halberstadt also helped out with photographs and advice, as did Ron Hare, Geoff Swanberg, Jim Mesko, Dean and Nancy Kleffman, David Hansen, Huck Hagenbuch, Karl Vonder Linden, Linda Johnson, and Kathy Vinson. The Defense Visual Information Center, the National Archives, and Real War Photos also supplied pictures.

Active duty and retired Marine Corps officers that made an extra effort in assisting the authors in the completion of this work include Lieutenant Colonels Gene Berbaum (Ret.) and John Quigley Active-duty Marine Corps majors that assisted the authors include Mark Johnson, Daryl Crane and Paul Webb. Marine Corps captains that assisted the authors include Jarel Heil, Ted Wong, Josh Smith, Robert Crum II, Bill Pelletier, and Chad Walton. Retired Marine Corps Warrant Officer "Gunner" Carroll was also very generous with his time in assisting the authors. Marine Corps noncommissioned officers that assisted the authors include Gunnery Sergeant Michael Dougherty, First Sergeant Scott DeCarrillo, Staff Sergeant Bryan Reed, and Sergeants Daniella Bacon and Jennie Haskamp.

A special note of thanks also goes to Gunnery Sergeant (Ret.) Thomas E. Williams (director of the United States Marine Corps Historical Company) for his assistance.

Introduction

This book is a very broad overview of most of the weapons now in use by the U.S. Marine Corps. It also includes some of the background history on the weapons that preceded those currently in service and profiles some new upcoming weapons. While most of the corps' weapons result from developmental work done by the other armed services, there are some ground and aerial weapons that are unique to the corps.

To understand the relationship between the weapons used by marines and the placement of those weapons in the corps, it is important to understand the general organization of the corps. At the top of the Marine Corps pyramid is Headquarters, U.S. Marine Corps (HQMC). Under it are two major subordinate commands, the Marine Corps Operating Forces and the Marine Corps Supporting Establishment. Most of the weapon-equipped elements of the Marine Corps are in the Marine Corps Operating Forces. The Marine Corps Supporting Establishment trains, maintains, and supports the operating forces.

The Marine Corps Operating Forces consist of three different elements: the Marine Security Forces, the Marine Security Guard Detachments, and the Fleet Marine Forces (FMF). The Marine Security Forces consist of about 3,400 personnel. They are tasked with guarding U.S. Navy shore stations. Marine Security Guard Detachments are assigned to U.S. embassies around the globe and number about 2,000 personnel.

Most weapon-equipped marines are in one of two FMFs. One is assigned to the navy's Pacific Fleet Command and the other to the navy's Atlantic Fleet Command. Each FMF includes a headquarters unit, elements of the service support (logistics) command, and any number of marine divisions and aircraft wings.

Today's Marine Corps has three active-duty marine divisions numbered one through three. They have a table of organization (TO&E) on paper calling for about 16,000 personnel each. In actual practice the number of men and women assigned to each division can vary from anywhere between 10,000 to 24,000 personnel.

The primary mission of the Marine Corps divisions is performing large-scale amphibious assault operations supported by marine aviation assets as well as U.S. Navy forces. They also can operate on land for a limited amount of time when reinforced. The Marine Corps also has a single non-activated reserve division assigned the number four. There are currently about 175,000 active-duty marines and about 99,000 reservists.

A marine division consists of a headquarters battalion, three infantry regiments and an artillery regiment. It also includes reconnaissance, tank, assault-amphibian, light armored reconnaissance, and combat engineer battalions. The three infantry regiments of 3,500 men each are the basic tactical (combat) units that the division performs its assigned missions with. A marine infantry regiment is composed of a headquarters company and three infantry battalions. Each battalion in turn is composed of a headquarters and service company that oversees and supports three rifle companies and a

weapon company. The rifle companies number about 200 men each, while the weapon company have a personnel strength of roughly 150.

Marine divisions do not deploy as separate combat entities as do army divisions since they lack the needed organic aviation and combat service support units. Rather, the corps will pull the manpower and equipment from its divisions to form various sized combat units depending on mission requirements. These are reinforced with aviation and combat service supports units. Once these combined arms units merge, they form marine air-ground task forces" (MAGTF).

There are a several different sized MAGTFs in the corps. No matter what their size they consist of four major components that include a command element (CE), a ground combat element (GCE), an aviation combat element (ACE), and a Combat Service Supports Element (CSSE).

The largest MAGTF organization appears as the marine expeditionary force (MEF) and may consist of up to 50,000 personnel. It is the main war-fighting organization in the Marine Corps. The ground combat element of a MEF is normally a single marine division reinforced with various combat support units. There are now three permanent MEFs existing in the corps, numbered one through three. Either a major general or a lieutenant general commands them.

One step down from the MEF is the temporary-task organized marine expeditionary brigade (MEB), which is normally commanded by a brigadier general. The MEB is composed of ground and aviation units detached from a parent MEF for a particular mission. Unlike the MEF the MEB does not have an organic command element and relies on its parent MEB for needed command personnel. It normally consists of about 14,000 personnel and is capable of conducting a limited degree of sustained air-ground operations. When its missions are finished, it is reabsorbed back into its parent MEF.

For missions less than war the Marine Corps depends on an air-ground combat task force called the marine expeditionary unit (MEU) special operations capable (SOC). They consist of about 2,200 marines commanded by a colonel. There are currently seven MEU (SOC) formations in the Marine Corps. Three are based at Camp Lejeune, North Carolina, and three are at Camp Pendleton, California. The remaining MEU (SOC) calls the Japanese island of Okinawa home.

A recent addition to the Marine Corps organization is the special purpose marine air-ground task force (SPMAGTF). It can vary in size, but is normally at least the size of a MEU (SOC) or a little bit smaller. Unlike a MEU (SOC) a SPMAGTF is a temporary-task organized unit created for a single purpose of a very limited duration. The men and equipment used to form a SPMAGTF come from a parent MEF. When a mission stands completed its personnel and equipment are reabsorbed back into the parent MEF.

A LITTLE BIT OF EVERYTHING: SMALL ARMS, EDGED WEAPONS, GRENADES AND MINES

United States Marine Corps Historical Company members are pictured with M1 rifles during a living history demonstration. They are wearing reproduction World War II-era Marine Corps uniforms. The M1 was the world's first self-loading (semiautomatic) rifle placed into widespread military service. It provided marine infantrymen with a firepower advantage against Japanese infantrymen still armed with bolt-action rifles. United States Marine Corps Historical Company

The various weapons used by the United States Marine Corps have evolved over the years to reflect both changes in fighting doctrine and advancements in weapon designs. Throughout this time it has been the individual rifleman who has always been the centerpiece of the corps' fighting power. Till this day the Marine Corps maintains that every marine is a rifleman before all other roles. This feeling is best reflected in the creed of the corps written by a marine general following the Japanese attack on Pearl Harbor, Hawaii, on December 7, 1941:

Above: **A Marine Corps range coach stands next to a recruit as he fires his bolt-action M1903 Springfield rifle. The recruit is using the tangent-leaf rear sight mounted above the barrel. This feature did not appear on later models of the Springfield rifle. Another spotting feature of this version of the Springfield rifle series was the straight stock. Later models had a pistol-grip-type stock.** U.S. Marine Corps

"This is my rifle. There are many like it, but this one is mine. My rifle is my best friend. It is my life. I must master it as I master my life.

My rifle without me is useless. Without my rifle, I am useless. I must fire my rifle true. I must shoot straighter than my enemy who is trying to kill me. I must shoot him before he shoots me. I will...

My rifle and myself know that what counts in this war is not the rounds we fire, the noise of our burst, nor the smoke we make. We know that it is the hits that count. We will hit...

My rifle is human, even as I, because it is my life. Thus, I will learn it as a brother. I will learn its weakness, its strength, its parts, its accessories, its sights, and its barrel. I will ever guard it against the ravages of weather and damage. I will keep my rifle clean and ready, even as I am clean and ready. We will become part of each other. We will...

Before God I swear this creed. My rifle and myself are the defenders of my country. We are the masters of our enemy. We are the saviors of my life. So be it, until there is no enemy, but Peace!"

From the 1920s until 1942, marine infantrymen carried various versions of the .30-caliber M1903 rifle, better known as the 03 Springfield. The term caliber describes the diameter of a weapon's bore. The ammunition fired from the M1903 rifle weapon was the 30-06. The 30 referred to the caliber of the ammunition (0.308-inch) and the 06 the year (1906) it entered military service.

The 03 Springfield was a bolt-action rifle with a five-round integral magazine. In the hands of a well-trained marine rifleman its accuracy was legendary. The final version of the 03 Springfield in Marine Corps service was the A3 version. Despite being replaced as the standard weapon in marine rifle squads during World War II, the corps kept a modified version of the 03 Springfield in service as a sniper rifle until the Korean War.

The replacement for the 03 Springfield in 1942 was a new rifle designated the M1, which fired the same .30-caliber round as the 03 Springfield. The M1 rifle was also known as the Garand after its designer, John C. Garand, chief civilian ordnance department engineer at the Springfield Armory. The M1 Garand rifle was a semiautomatic, gas-operated weapon, that weighed about 9 1/2 pounds.

Fully loaded, the M1 held eight rounds secured in a metal clip that was loaded as a single unit into the top of the weapon's receiver. The empty clip ejected with the last empty cartridge case with a loud clang. This was a sore point with many marines, since it announced to the enemy that they just ran out of ammunition. Another sore point with some marines was the fact that the weapon could not be topped off with extra rounds. Despite these design shortcomings, the M1 Garand was a tough and reliable weapon that was far superior to the bolt-action rifles used by opponents of the United States. Some M1 Garands continue to see service for drill and ceremonial use in the corps till this day.

M14 RIFLE

The M1 Garand rifle remained in corps service until it was replaced in the late 1950s by the M14 rifle, which fired a 7.62mm (0.308 inch) cartridge. The 7.62mm cartridge was the same caliber as the 30-06 cartridge used in U.S. military small arms since World War I, but shorter. Despite being shorter, the 7.62mm ammunition possessed operational parameters that generally matched, or in some cases surpassed, the old 30-06 ammunition. This was possible because of post-World War II advancements in ammunition propellant technology. The advantage of shorter ammunition was that it gave manufacturers the ability to design small arms, from rifles to machine guns, with shorter receivers, making them more compact.

The M14 was nothing more than an updated and modified version of the M1 Garand. When originally designed the weapon had a select-fire capability, meaning it could be fired in either semiautomatic or in full-automatic mode. The U.S. military quickly added a selector shaft lock on its inventory of M14 rifles so that only the semi-automatic fire mode was opperational. Instead of firing from an eight-round internal clip as with the M1 Garand, the M14 fed from a detachable 20-round box magazine that inserted into the bottom of the weapon's receiver. The M14 rifle had a maximum effective range of 500 yards.

Production of the M14 ended in January 1963, although it continued to serve the corps until the early 1970s. About 700 modified M14 rifles were used by marines as sniper rifles during the Vietnam War. They remained in the inventory until the late 1980s. Some M14s

continue to see service for drill and ceremonial use in the corps today, and others appear in competitive marksmanship matches sponsored by the military.

In 1989, the Marine Corps began a program to convert some of its remaining inventory of M14 rifles into a new weapon called the designated marksman rifle (DMR). The DMR boasts a new barrel and a fiberglass stock. It also features a 10-power scope and a folding bipod. The DMRs were originally fielded to fleet antiterrorism teams (FASTs) and explosive ordnance disposal (EOD) units. They also now serve in the Marine Corps' recently formed terrorism and force protection (AT/FB) units. Performing the ongoing process of converting M14 rifles into DMRs is the precision weapon section (PWS) of the Marine Corps, which used to be called the rifle team equipment (RTE) shop.

Left: **A small number of M14 rifles remaining in Marine Corps inventory see use in a corps-wide marksmanship program called Competition in Arms. Pictured is Master Sergeant Arthur Onspaugh, a member of the Marine Corps rifle team, taking aim with his match-grade M14 rifle during a high-power-rifle competition conducted at Camp Perry, Ohio, by the National Rifle Association every July and August.** Defense Visual Information Center

Above: **The Marine Corps' newly introduced designated marksman rifle (DMR) is an upgraded and improved version of the M14. To create the DMR, Marine Corps weapon experts took an older match-grade M14 rifle barrel and receiver and mounted them on a modern fiberglass stock that offers the shooter an ergonomic pistol grip. The DMR also comes with a sound suppressor on the end of the barrel of the weapon pictured.** Sergeant Andrew D. Pomykal

A young marine armed with an M16A2 rifle carefully watches his surroundings while on the radio. This picture was taken on April 9, 2003, during Operation Iraqi Freedom. The marine pictured belonged to Echo Company, Battalion Landing Team, Second Battalion, Second Marines Twenty-fourth MEU, and was taking part in his unit's seizing of an airfield once held by the Iraqi Tenth Armored Division in Al Amarah, Iraq.
Corporal Jeff Sisto

Most marines who saw service during the Vietnam War eventually had their M14 rifles replaced with smaller and lighter M16 rifles. Like the M14 rifle that it replaced, the M16 was magazine fed, gas operated, and designed for either semiautomatic or full-automatic fire. Gone was the traditional polished-wood stock that marines had long been accustomed to. In its place was a lightweight black plastic fiberglass stock.

Due to the smaller and less powerful 5.56mm caliber cartridge for the M16, the normal range setting for the rear sight was between zero and 330 yards. Adjustments for ranges beyond 330 yards were possible, although at these extended ranges accuracy was doubtful. This limitation was not as serious as one might assume, since battlefield statistics kept by the U.S. Army since World War I show that most battlefield kills from small-arms fire occurred at less than 300 yards. Ammunition was fed to the M16 via a detachable 20-round box magazine inserted

into the lower receiver. Later a 30-round box magazine was developed for the gun, which is now the standard for all M16-series weapons.

The combat debut of the M16 rifle in the army and the marines was badly marred by the fact that the weapon quickly developed a slew of serious operational problems. Almost all of them could be attributed to the Department of Defense's (DOD) mismanagement of the weapon's development, production, and fielding. Thousands of complaints from U.S. servicemen soon forced Congress to take a long, hard look at the DOD's stewardship of the M16 rifle program. Under congressional glare, the DOD quickly set about correcting the M16's problems. An improved version of the M16 rifle designated the M16A1, entered army and marine service in 1967. It quickly established a reputation in combat as a reliable and effective killing tool.

While the M16A1 rifle performed admirably for the corps during the Vietnam War, some deficiencies were noted during field use including the weapon's lack of longer-range accuracy. To correct the M16A1's deficiencies negotiations between the U.S. military and Colt Industries began in September 1979. The goal was to develop a product-improved version of the M16A1. Firing tests of an improved model began the next year, with formal adoption of the weapon, designated the M16A2, by the marines in 1984.

Improvements to the M16A2 rifle included a change in rifling and a heavier, stiffer barrel. This was combined with a heavier bullet with more grains of powder. All these factors led to much greater accuracy at longer ranges than had proved possible with the M16A1 rifle. According to the Marine Corps, the maximum effective range of an M16A2 rifle firing at a point target is 600

A marine infantryman wearing a protective mask takes aim with his M16 rifle. This was the first version of a weapon that continues to see service with the Marine Corps today. An identifying feature of the M16 rifle is the three-prong flash suppressor seen on the weapon pictured. The designer of the M16 was Eugene Stoner, a former marine, who began designing rifles after his discharge from the corps at the end of World War II. Defense Visual Information Center

Marine infantrymen fire at enemy snipers with their M16A1 rifles during the Vietnam War. An empty cartridge case is visible after being ejected from the weapon in the foreground. Both M16A1 rifles pictured have the original 20-round detachable magazines. Spotting features for the M16A1 include a new flash suppressor and the addition of a forward bolt-assist device that projects from the upper rear part of the weapon's receiver. Jim Mesko collection

Two marines armed with M16A2 rifles maintain their position during a field training exercise. The M16A2 rifle was fitted with new, sturdier, ribbed tubular hand guards visible on the weapons pictured. They not only offered the operator better forward control of the weapon, but provided better heat dissipation than the triangular-sectioned hand guards fitted on the M16 and M16A1. Defense Visual Information Center

yards. For engaging area targets, the weapon's effective range increases to 880 yards. Other improvements to the M16A2 included a burst-control device that limited automatic fire to a maximum of three rounds per trigger pull. It also featured redesigned, interchangeable hand-guard halves and a new muzzle brake compensator to reduce the rise or jump of the muzzle during burst fire.

M16 RIFLE UPGRADES

This picture of a marine armed with an M16A2 rifle demonstrates the jury-rigged arrangement needed to attach a passive night sight to the weapon's integral carrying handle. Removing the night sight from the handle and adding other types of optical devices under combat conditions would not be an easy task. This helped to push the army and marines to adopt new versions of the M16 series of rifles with an adapter rail located under a removable carrying handle. With the adapter rail, a rifleman could easily mount and dismount any sighting device fitted with rail grabbers.
Defense Visual Information Center

By the early 1990s, the army had identified a need to update the M16A2's ability to more easily accept a variety of accessories and optics. Up to this point, devices added to the M16A2 rifle (such as optical devices) had to be either strapped to the weapon with tape, plastic tie-down straps, or jury-rigged with a screw-type mechanism attached to the weapon's integral carrying handle. This arrangement remains standard practice for army and marine infantrymen still equipped with the M16A2 rifle. To correct this unsatisfactory situation, the army began a development program in 1993 called the modular weapon system (MWS), in which the Marine Corps joined from the outset. At the conclusion of the program in 1998, the army adopted two new versions of the M16 series designated the M4 and M4A1 carbines. The marines adopted three new versions of the M16 series varying numbers, the M4 and M4A1 carbines as well as the M16A4 rifle.

The M4 carbine and the M16A4 rifle can fire either semiautomatic or three-round-burst mode via a selector switch. The M4A1 carbine, also referred to as the close-quarter battle weapon (CQBW), has a different trigger mechanism, allowing the weapon to be fired in either semiautomatic or full-automatic mode via a selector switch. The M4 carbine and the M4A1 CQBW have a retractable butt-stock with various intermediate stop positions. The M16A4 rifle retained the fixed butt-stock seen on the M16A2 rifle.

All three versions of the M16 rifle adopted by the Marine Corps under the MWS program also have removable carrying handles under which is found an adapter rail affixed to the top of the weapon's receiver. This adapter rail allows the attachment of a variety of daytime optical-sighting systems and night-vision equipment when they are equipped with rail grabbers. All earlier versions of the M16 rifle, including the M16A1 and M16A2 variants, have an integral carrying handle.

The M16A4 rifle retains the tubular ribbed front hand guards found on the M16A2 rifle. In contrast, some examples of the M4 carbine and all production examples of the M4A1 CQBW are fitted with a device called the rail interface system (RIS). A newer version of the RIS, the rail adapter system (RAS), was recently introduced. Despite their fancy names, they are nothing more than a new type of front hand guard that includes adapter rails on their top, sides, and bottom, allowing a variety of devices such as laser aiming devices or flashlights with rail grabbers to be attached to the weapon. They differ in the manner in which they are attached to a weapon and the types of barrels they can be used with.

Of the three versions of the M16 series approved by the Marine Corps under the MWS program, the first to enter service in 1999 was the M4A1 CQBW. It saw issue to Marine Corps force reconnaissance units, fleet antiterrorism teams, and military police special response teams. Since that time, the M4A1 CQBW has also begun to appear in Marine Corps light armored vehicle (LAV) units. Since the corps could not decide if the M4 carbine or the M16A4 rifle was the better choice for infantry units, it conducted a series of tests to compare the two weapons. These tests were completed in 2002, and the corps chose to acquire the M16A4 rifle over the M4 carbine. Fielding of the M16A4 rifle began just prior to Operation Iraqi Freedom in 2003 and will continue to selectively replace some M16A2s in marine infantry battalions for several years.

Currently, only a limited number of M4 carbines are in service with the corps pending a corps-wide procurement policy. A small number are with the RIS and have been supplied to helicopter gunship crews. Another version issued in small numbers has shortened, tubular-ribbed front hand guards as seen on the M16A2 rifle that do not allow accessories attachment, since there are no integral adapter rails. Also, some leftover test versions of various configurations of the M4 carbine have found their way to field units.

The M4 and M4A1 CQBW were not the first carbines in marine service. During World War II, the corps used the .30-caliber M1 carbine. While the bore of the weapon was the same as the M1 Garand, it fired a completely different type of round that was both shorter and far less powerful than the 30-06 round fired from the M1.

The M1 carbine was a gas-operated, semiautomatic weapon for use by officers and noncommissioned officers, as well as marines not equipped with rifles. Ammunition was fed to the gun via a detachable 15-round box magazine inserted into the lower receiver. Due to unreliability and poor stopping power, the M1 proved extremely unpopular with many marines. After World War II, the marines adopted an improved version, designated the M2 that had the provision for full-automatic fire. Because of the higher rate of fire, the M2 used a detachable 30-round box magazine. Both the M1 and M2 carbines were in service with the corps in limited numbers until the Korean War.

Marine Sergeant Kris Floyd is pictured firing an M4 carbine during a training exercise. The smaller size of the weapon is clearly apparent when compared to the M16A2 rifle being fired by the marine in the background. Like the new M16A4 rifle and the M4A1 carbine, the M4 carbine has an adapter rail affixed to the top of the weapon's receiver to mount a variety of optical sighting devices. The detachable carrying handle seen in this picture covers the adapter rail when not in use. Corporal Paula M. Fitzgerald

Marine Corps Sergeant A. Lara is pictured cleaning his M1 carbine during the Vietnam War. Since the M1 was no longer in service with the Marine Corps then, Sgt. Lara no doubt acquired his weapon in trade with a South Vietnamese soldier. Unlike handguns, which tend to have an effective range of no more than 25 yards, the M1 carbine could deliver accurate fire up to 300 yards. Jim Mesko collection

At the end of every Marine Corps rifle is an attachment for a bayonet. From the beginning of the twentieth century until early World War II, the standard-issue bayonet was designated the M1905. It had an impressive 16-inch blade that was impractical in most situations. The army and marines soon opted for a shorter bayonet with a 10-inch blade designated the M1. Production of the M1 bayonet began in April 1943 and continued until August 1945, with over two million manufactured. For the M1 carbine a smaller bayonet with a 6.75-inch blade was first produced in July 1944. It was designated M4 bayonet-knife and was based on the army's World War II M3 trench knife.

With the introduction of the M14 rifle into army and marine service in the late 1950s, a new bayonet entered into use that had a 6.75 inch blade and was designated the M7 bayonet. When the first version of the M16 rifle entered U.S. military service, the corps adapted the M7 bayonet to the weapon. It continues to be used by the corps. In 2003, the Marine Corps placed its first order for a new multipurpose bayonet with an 8-inch blade. It will replace the M7 bayonet, as well as the famous KA-BAR fighting and utility knife from World War II. A spotting feature of the new multipurpose bayonet has a small hole near the tip of the blade.

The World War II-era KA-BAR and its modern descendents have a 7-inch blade. The knife is designated the Mark 2 by the navy. While manufactured by several different contractors during World War II the major builder was Union Cutlery Company of Olean, New York,

A marine infantryman attaches a new M9 multipurpose bayonet to the muzzle end of his M16A2 rifle during Operation Iraqi Freedom in 2003. The Marine Corps has always stressed the importance of every marine mastering the use of the bayonet, despite historical documentation that shows that very few enemy soldiers ever die of bayonet wounds. However, the corps believes that training young marines in the use of the bayonet will make them more aggressive. Corporal Jeff Sisto

Pictured in its leather scabbard on a marine's hip is a Mark 2 KA-BAR knife. Made from cold steel sheets, every KA-BAR passes through a long process of hardening and tempering so it can resist breaking under the most severe pressure. The handle on the KA-BAR is made from 22 slotted leather discs compressed under great pressure which transforms them into a solid unit that will resist moisture of any kind. Michael Green

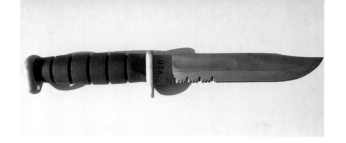

The Mark II KA-BAR is 12 inches long, with a 7-inch blade. While the KA-BAR is generally classified as a fighting knife, the number of enemy soldiers actually killed with the weapon is extremely small. Like the various bayonets in use with the corps since World War II, the KA-BAR normally performs the role of utility knife for everything from opening food ration cans to digging foxholes. Michael Green

A marine on board the flight deck of a naval ship is pictured firing an M4A1 carbine, also known as the close quarter battle weapon (CQBW). He has mounted an optical sighting device on the adapter rail affixed to the top of the weapon's receiver. The marine is holding the forward handgrip nicknamed the broomstick, which attaches to the bottom adapter rail on the weapon's hand guard. Staff Sergeant Brian Reed

which stamped each knife with their firm's trademark name KA-BAR. Marines were soon calling all Mark 2 knifes KA-BARS regardless of manufacturer, and this nickname has survived to this day. Despite the introduction of the new multipurpose bayonet, the KA-BAR will no doubt survive in marine service for many years to come.

Below: **The Thompson submachine gun that saw service with the Marine Corps in World War II came in several different versions. The first to enter service in 1928 was designated the M1921, later changed to M1928A1. During World War II its replacement was a simplified version called the M1. The final version of this famous weapon was the M1A1, as seen in this picture. Over 500,000 examples came off the assembly lines in 1943 and 1944.** Michael Green

One of the best-known American submachine guns to see service in World War II was the Thompson, which was a compact, full-automatic blow back weapon that fired a short-range .45-caliber pistol cartridge. Several progressively improved versions were placed into service during the war. In early versions, ammunition was fed to the gun, via a detachable 50-round drum magazine or a 20-round box magazine, which was inserted into the lower receiver. Later models were restricted to using either a detachable 20- or 30-round box magazine.

Because the Thompson was both costly and time consuming to build, the army's ordnance department tried to replace it with the cheaper and easier-to-build .45-Caliber M3 submachine guns. Like the Thompson, the grease gun was a full-blow-back-operated weapon. An improved model of the grease gun, designated the M3A1 submachine gun, came out at the end of the war. Ammunition was fed to the gun via a detachable 30-round box magazine inserted into the lower receiver.

The Thompson and the grease gun were used by tank crews, military policemen, and mortar- and machine-gun-squad leaders. The guns were also used by parachute units (disbanded during World War II) and raider units which were early forerunners of current divisional-level reconnaissance units better known as recon units. The Thompson lasted in service with the corps until the Korean War. The grease gun remained in the corps inventory with tank units until the 1970s.

The first foreign-made submachine gun put into Marine Corps service was the compact and reliable German-designed-and-built MP-5N Heckler and Koch 9mm submachine gun. As with all submachine guns the

SUBMACHINE GUNS

A firing line of marines takes aim with their M4A1 CQBWs during target practice. The front hand guard on the weapon in the foreground differs from those in the background. Instead of being mounted inside the hand guards and accessed through vertical slots, as with the M4A1 CQBW in the background, the adapter rails on the M4A1 CQBW in the foreground are on the exterior of the hand guard. U.S. Marine Corps

GRENADES

The M67 fragmentation hand grenade is the standard in the corps today. Like all hand grenades, it can be extremely dangerous to the enemy, and the thrower unless he uses extreme caution. When throwing hand grenades, marines must be very aware of any intervening obstacles such as walls, trees, and vines so the grenade doesn't bounce back to the thrower. Hans Halberstadt

short barrel length of the weapon meant that accuracy was restricted to short-range combat engagements. The weapon could be fired in single-shot mode or on full-automatic mode. Ammunition was fed to the gun via a detachable 30-round box magazine inserted into the lower receiver.

The MP-5N, like the World War II-era Thompson and grease gun, was not an infantry-squad-level weapon. It was a close-quarters-battle (CQB) weapon used by corps special operation units and marines involved in antiterrorism and security duties. Despite the MP-5N's excellent reputation, it was replaced in 1999 with a new weapon because its maximum effective range was less than 110 years, and its 9mm rounds no longer had the stopping power to penetrate modern body armor. It also did not have any integral provisions to mount the large number of accessories now considered essential to many marine missions.

The chosen successor to the MP-5N in corps service was the M4A1 close-quarter-battle weapon (CQBW). Like the MP-5N, the CQBW has an optional sound suppressor. The maximum effective range of the CQBW against point targets is 550 yards, and 800 yards for area targets. Because the CQBW has the same adapter rails as the M16A4 rifle and the M4 carbine, as well as the RIS, many devices such as laser pointers, flashlights, optics, etc. can be mounted on the weapon. While these add-on devices greatly increase the weapon's effectiveness in a variety of tactical settings, they also change the weapon's center of gravity. To compensate for this, there is a forward handle (called a broomstick) on the CQBW giving the operator a better grasp on the weapon when firing. Furthermore, because a number of add-on devices may also be fitted under the front hand guards, the operator may not have any place to put his hands to steady the weapon. The broom stick gives the operator a place to hold on to the front of the CQBW.

Hand grenades are nothing more than small hand-thrown bombs. They supplement small-arms fire in close-combat situations. The Marine Corps has used many types of hand grenades since World War I. These included fragmentation, offensive, chemical, practice, and training grenades. The most common are the fragmentation grenades that contain an explosive charge in a body that shatters into small pieces on detonation.

In World War I the Marine Corps used a copy of a French-army-designed fragmentation hand grenade with a serrated cast-iron body and high-explosive filler. Designated the Mk. II by the U.S., it was better known by its nickname, the pineapple grenade, since its serrated body reminded soldiers of the tropical fruit. The 21-ounce

grenade had a maximum distance of about 40 yards when thrown by someone with a strong arm. Upon explosion it produced about 50 lethal fragments.

During World War II, the marines used an improved version of the Mk. II hand grenade. The newer version weighed 22.4 ounces and featured better-quality, high-explosive fillers that produced a greater quality of lethal fragments when detonated. The Mk. II hand grenade remained in Marine Corps front-line service through the Korean War, and was used as a training grenade for marines before deployment overseas during the Vietnam War. The M26 and M33 fragmentation grenades replaced the MK. II in the mid-1960s. The new hand grenades featured smooth sheet-metal bodies and a serrated wire coil in the body that broke into many fragments upon detonation. Both types had an effective casualty radius of about 17 yards.

The M61 and M67 replaced the M26 and M33 series fragmentation grenades in corps service in the late 1980s. The M61 weighs 16 ounces and has a thin sheet-metal body that contains 5.5 ounces of explosives. It also has a serrated wire coil in the grenade body that breaks into many fragments upon detonation. The M67 weighs 14 ounces and has a steel-sphere body that contains 6.5 ounces of high explosives. Both grenades have an effective casualty radius of about 17 yards. Like all U.S. hand grenades since World War I, once you remove the safety pin ring and release the safety lever, there is only a 4- to 5-second delay before it explodes.

GRENADE LAUNCHERS

To load the M203 40mm grenade launcher, the operator pushes the barrel of the launcher forward and then slides a round into the weapon's breech as pictured. Once the soldier completes that motion, he pulls the barrel of the weapon rearwards. This action locks the weapon shut and prepares it for firing. Defense Visual Information Center

A young marine is pictured with an M16A2 rifle equipped with an M203 40mm grenade launcher mounted underneath the barrel of the weapon. The unloaded launcher unit weighs only 3 pounds. To attach the M203 to the M16A2 rifle calls for the use of a special set of square-shaped hand guards, seen in this picture.
Hans Halberstadt

Marines prepare to return fire at Iraqi troops during Operation Iraqi Freedom. Two of the three marines pictured have M16A2 rifles fitted with the M203 40mm grenade launcher. For target engagements at the maximum range of the weapon, the operator uses a quadrant sight that attaches to the left side of an M16A2 carrying handle. The sight is graduated in various increments ranging from 55 yards to 440 yards. Corporal Jeff Sisto

Because the effective range of hand grenades remains limited by the ability of the individual thrower, there have been many efforts over the years to extend the range that an infantryman can engage a target with his grenades. In World War I, the army's ordnance department copied a French army grenade launcher known as the Vivien Bessier (VB).

A rifle grenade launcher consists of a metal tube attached to the muzzle of a rifle that remains in place with a locking device or clamp. The launcher holds and positions the grenade for firing. The gaseous energy generated by firing a blank cartridge propels the grenade from the launcher. Special sights assist in aiming rifle grenades since they have an arching trajectory in flight.

The American copy of the French VB grenade launcher would remain in service with the army and the marines until the 1920s. It was replaced with the M1 grenade launcher designed for use with the 03 Springfield rifle. As the M1 Garand replaced the 03 Springfield in U.S. military service during World War II, the army's ordnance department designed a new grenade launcher for the M1 Garand designated the M7 grenade launcher. The M1 carbine got the M8 grenade launcher. Antitank, antipersonnel, and smoke grenades could be used with the M7 and M8 grenade launchers.

The M76 grenade launcher was used on the M14 rifle as it began to replace the M1 Garand in army and marine service. None of the grenade launchers were truly satisfactory, since once attached to their respective weapons, the weapons could no longer function in semiautomatic mode. To overcome the tactical limitations imposed on army rifle squads by restricting one of its weapons to fire only single shots when fitted with a grenade launcher, the army began developing a dedicated squad-level grenade launcher in the late 1950s. The new weapon would fill the void between the maximum throwing distance of a hand grenade and the shortest range of supporting mortar fire. The result of this effort was the fielding of the 40mm M79 grenade launcher in marine service in the early 1960s.

Looking much like a sawed-off shotgun, the M79 was a single-shot, shoulder-fired weapon with a maximum effective range of about 440 yards. Like an old-fashioned hunting shotgun the weapon broke open for loading a 40mm grenade round into the breech. Due to the sound it made when fired, U.S. soldiers nicknamed it the bloop gun during the Vietnam War. Infantryman assigned to the M79 were normally armed only with only a pistol for close-range, self-defense use.

Although the M79 was well regarded by the U.S. troops that used it in combat, the army decided that the loss of firepower in an infantry squad by assigning men to only operate the M79 was unacceptable. The army set out to develop a new type of grenade launcher in 1967 that attached to the M16A1 rifle without interfering with the weapon's ability to fire in semiautomatic mode. AAI Corporation, under the direction of army weapon's command eventually created the successor to the M79, called the 40mm M203 grenade launcher.

In the early 1970s, the 40mm M203 grenade launcher entered Marine Corps service. It is a lightweight (3 pounds) stubby little device that is small enough to fit under a specially designed pair of front handgrips on the M16A1 and later the M16A2 rifle. Like earlier rifle grenades, the M203 has a special sighting device that compensates for the arching trajectory of 40mm grenades in flight. The maximum effective range for the M203 with point targets is roughly 163 yards. With area targets, the maximum effective range of the M203 is almost 383 yards.

A variety of ammunition types are available for the M203, including a high-explosive (HE) round. The grenade or explosive element in the projectile is formed by wrapping a notched, rectangular-shaped steel wire around a high-explosive filler. When the round detonates, more than 325 fragments appear, although the effective casualty radius is only 5 1/2 yards. Other types of 40mm grenade rounds designed for the M203 include a white star parachute round that will burn for 40 seconds with an intensity of 45,000 candle power and a white star cluster round that will burn for 7 seconds at 55,000 candle power. For extremely close-range engagements within 38 yards, a multi-projectile round for the M203 contains 20-twenty grain pellets each (about the size of #4 buckshot).

Forty-millimeter grenades designed for the M203 include a tear-gas grenade with a maximum range of about 440 yards that will burn and release gas for about 25 seconds after impact. There is also an HE air-burst round that bounces about 6 feet in the air after it hits the ground and then explodes. For combat with armored targets, the M203 has an HE dual-purpose round that can penetrate 2 inches of steel plate.

Handguns

While many different types of revolvers have seen service with the corps over many decades, the most common handgun from 1925 until the mid-1980s was the pistol, automatic (a misnomer) caliber model M1911A1. It was also better known as the .45 or the .45 automatic, since the weapon fired a very large and powerful .45-caliber bullet that had a great deal of knockdown power. Since the Colt Patent Firearms Company had a degree of involvement in the early development and production of the weapon, it has also commonly been called the Colt .45 or just the Colt.

A vehicle commander of an amphibious assault vehicle (AAV) wears a leather shoulder holster containing a Beretta M9 pistol. The crews of wheeled and tracked armored fighting vehicles have always favored wearing pistols, since their compact size allows them to be carried on their person. Defense Visual Information Center

The M1911A1 was a semiautomatic, recoil-operated, magazine-fed, self-loading, pistol normally carried by officers, noncommissioned officers, and marines not armed with a rifle. As with all military pistols, the M1911A1 entered service as a close-range self-defense weapon. The ammunition was housed in a seven-round detachable box magazine that inserted into the weapon's handgrip. The M1911A1 weighed 3 pounds loaded and had a maximum effective range of about 55 yards in the hands of a trained shooter.

This photo compares the M1911A1 pistol to its replacement in Marine Corps service, the Beretta M9 pistol. It takes a great deal of practice to maintain any degree of proficiency in using the M9, as is the case with all pistols. Befitting their role as self-defense weapons, pistols are generally weapons of last resort. With the introduction of the M9 in 1986, the corps revised its pistol qualification course to make it more realistic. It now includes a variety of targets that call for engagement successfully from different ranges and from different firing postures and positions. Defense Visual Information Center

The single-action M1911A1 remained the Marine Corps' main handgun until it was replaced in 1985 by the double-action, Italian-designed Beretta M9 pistol that fired a 9mm round. Like the M1911A1, the Beretta is a semiautomatic, recoil-operated, magazine-fed weapon. The two pistons differ in that the Beretta is lighter at only 2.55 pounds and has a magazine capacity of 15 rounds. Unlike the M1911A1, the Beretta is also an ambidextrous weapon that allows both right- and left-handed shooters

Marine Corps Sergeant M. W. Patrick, a military policeman, is in the prone firing position and using a log for protection during a 200-hour training program for base military police personnel. He's taking aim at a target with an M1911A1 pistol, a simple, tough, and reliable weapon that proved itself in combat with marines around the globe since it was introduced into service after World War I. Defense Visual Information Center

to fire it with equal ease. The decision to adopt the foreign-designed Beretta pistol was based on the U.S. military's need to standardize its inventory of pistols with a weapon that fires the same 9mm ammunition used by NATO allies.

A small number of specially modified versions of the M1911A1 remain in corps service today with reconnaissance (recon) units attached to marine expeditionary units (MEUs) that are special operations capable (SOC). The modified weapons are designated 1911A1 MEU (SOC) pistols and differ greatly from the original M1911A1 pistols that were so familiar to earlier generations of marines. They have a precision barrel and trigger assembly along with a commercial competition-level ambidextrous safety. They also have extra-wide, rubber-coated safety grips, a rounded hammer spur and high-profile combat sights. In addition, a new stainless-steel, seven-round, competition-grade magazine with a rounded plastic follower, and an extended floor plate come with the weapon. The MEU (SOC) pistol also has the advantage of weighing only 2.5 pounds compared to the 3 pounds of the original M1911A1.

COMBAT SHOTGUNS

A shotgun team from a Marine Corps weapons-company prepares to fire simulated beanbag (non-lethal) rounds at aggressors during riot-control training conducted in Prizren, Kosovo, in conjunction with German army units. They are armed with a militarized version of the well-known Remington 870 Wingmaster 12-gauge (18.5mm) pump-action shotgun, designated the Remington M870 Mark 1 shotgun. Sergeant Zachary A. Bathon

During World War I, the Marine Corps put into service several civilian-designed shotguns that were modified for military use. These 12-gauge, manually operated (pump), repeating shotguns came from both Winchester and Remington. Modifications included ventilated hand guards for the Winchester shotguns and an adapter for mounting a bayonet on both companies weapons. The shotguns were called trench guns during the war. Shortly thereafter, they were called riot guns.

The World War I-era 12-gauge shotguns would last in corps service until shortly before the Japanese attack on Pearl Harbor, which brought the United States officially into World War II. To replace the aging and worn World War I-era shotguns, the army's ordnance department ordered militarized 12-gauge shotguns from a wide variety of builders for both the army and the corps. Guns came from Winchester, Stevens, Ithaca, Remington and Savage.

The World War II-era 12-gauge shotguns continued in use with the marines until the mid-1960s. By this time they were beginning to show their age. To replace them, the corps put into service several new militarized versions of commercially available 12-gauge shotguns from Remington, Winchester and Mossberg. The Remington shotgun, adopted by the marines, is a variation of the standard M870 shotgun and was the most popular gun in the service. The weapon is designated the Remington M870 Mark 1 and features a seven-cartridge extended tubular magazine under its barrel. With a plastic butt-plate and prominent finger grooves along its extended forearm of the weapon, the gun can also utilize a bayonet.

All weapons subjected to hard use eventually need to be replaced. By the late 1990s, the corps recognized that it needed to field replacements for all its various 12-gauge shotguns. Due to logistical concerns, the corps wanted to field only one type of shotgun to meet all its needs and obtained funding from Congress for the new shotgun. However, Congress soon ordered the corps to relinquish those funds to the new Joint Service Small Arms Program Office (JSSAP) and then ordered all the services to utilize only one type of shotgun. After conducting comparative trials, the services adopted a militarized, Benelli-made, 12-gauge weapon product designated the M1014 joint-service combat shotgun.

The M1014 has a telescoping butt-stock and the same accessory rail on top of the receiver as on the M16A4 rifle, the M4 carbine, the M4A1 CQBW, and the newer production examples of the M249 SAW. This feature allows the mounting of a wide variety of daytime

A member of a Marine Corps boarding team takes aim with his Remington M870 Mark 1 shotgun. It was during the Vietnam War that marine infantrymen rediscovered the value of the shotgun in the close confines of a jungle environment, where the enemy could be mere yards away in the dense underbrush. Besides firing a powerful buckshot load that could kill an enemy soldier out to 33 yards, several special flechette (steel dart) rounds were developed for army and marine Corps shotguns. Defense Visual Information Center

Marine Sergeant Alma L. Fragoso fires the new M1014 joint service combat shotgun during a range exercise. Like all female marines, Sergeant Fragoso must be as proficient with the entire assortment of marine small arms as any one marine. While female marines do not yet serve in corps ground combat elements such as armor or infantry they must prepare for the possibility that their command and support units may become targets for enemy forces. Sergeant Joseph Lee

optical sighting systems or night-vision equipment on the M1014. Unlike the manually operated (pump) repeating shotguns used by the corps since World War I, the M1014 has a semi-automatic, gas-operated action.

The M1014 is about 40 inches long with its telescoping butt-stock extended and only about 35 inches long in its collapsed position. A pistol grip may be added to assist in firing the gun. The M1014 weighs 8.44 pounds empty and has an ambidextrous manual cross bolt. The integral tubular magazine found under the weapon's barrel holds six cartridges that come loaded one at a time. When firing buckshot, the M1014 has an effective range of about 40 yards. When firing solid slugs, the M1014's effective range goes up to 100 yards.

When originally offered to the U.S. military, the M1014 was touted as being able to fire the entire range of non-lethal ammunition, which was in use with the marines. Unfortunately, this was not the case and was a disadvantage of auto-loading shotguns. This forced the marines to retain the Mossburg 500 and 500A2 shotguns in service for the purpose of employing the current inventory of non-lethal shotgun ammunition.

ANTIPERSONNEL MINES

Antipersonnel mines cause casualties in foot troops. They also protect antitank minefields and other obstacles and give local security and warning to defending units. Nuisance mines can be used to harass and delay advancing enemy forces. They cannot damage tracked and armored fighting vehicles, but they can damage non-armored wheeled vehicles. The explosive charges contained in modern antipersonnel mines range from 1 pound to 1 1/2 pounds; a weight of anywhere from 5 to 160 pounds can detonate an antipersonnel mine.

The best-known antipersonnel mine now in corps service is a Vietnam War-era design and is designated antipersonnel mine M18A1. It is better known by its popular nickname the Claymore. It is an above-ground, directional-fragmentation mine made from plastic that weighs only 3 1/2 pounds. When the Claymore detonates, a fan-shaped pattern of spherical steel fragments is projected in a 60-degree horizontal arc covering a casualty radius of 110 yards to a height of about 6 feet. Besides killing or wounding foot troops, the fragments will also puncture tires, gas tanks, crankcases, radiators, and engine accessories. The Claymore is detonated by an electrical or non-electrical command or by trip wire.

Another antipersonnel mine used by the marines is designated the M16A1 and bears the nickname Bouncing Betty. The roughly 7-pound mine gets its nickname from the fact that it's a bouncing fragmentation mine. Once activated, it pops out of the ground, rises to a height of 6 feet, and detonates. A pressure of between 8 and 20 will set off its 1-pound high-explosive content. The M16A1 is activated by a trip wire that attaches to the fuse's release pin ring.

MACHINE GUNS
AND SNIPER RIFLES

The gunner on a water-cooled Browning M1917A1 .30-caliber machine gun takes aim at Japanese positions during World War II. The water can for the weapon sits at the foot of the tripod. The hose that connects the water can to the water jacket surrounding the weapon's barrel is also visible. Because of the weight and size of the M1917A1, it was not a weapon that crews moved easily around the battlefield, particularly in a jungle environment. Real War Photos

During World War I, the army and the marines put into service a water-cooled, recoil-operated, .30-caliber machine gun invented by John M. Browning. It was designated the caliber .30 Browning machine gun model 1917, and it fired the same cartridge as the .03 Springfield and M1 Garand rifles. Its maximum effective rate of fire was 600 rounds per minute. Some minor improvements made to the World War I-era M1917s in the late 1930s led to the weapon's redesignation as the Browning machine gun caliber .30, M1917A1 heavy machine gun (HMG). The weapon was designated a heavy machine gun, because it was less mobile than other types of army and marine machine guns, not because of its weight.

Above: **Manning a Browning M1917A1 water-cooled .30-caliber machine gun during a public demonstration are two members of the Marine Corps Historical Company. Its membership consists of former and active-duty marines, although prior military service is not a requirement to join. Each member must buy their own uniforms and equipment and have a working knowledge of Marine Corps history, traditions, and culture that they can share with the public.** United States Marine Corps Historical Company

The M1917A1 did weigh (with water added) a total of 41 pounds. The tripod added another 53.4 pounds to the package. In addition, the three-man crew had to carry extra water and ammunition cans, plus some minor accessories. Until 1944, the M1917A1 heavy machine guns (HMG) belonged to heavy weapons companies of marine rifle battalions. When these units ceased to exist in 1944 their machine guns moved into rifle company heavy weapons platoons. The M1917A1 remained in army and marine service until the early 1960s.

To address the weight problem posed by the M1917A1, the army's ordnance department began studying a much lighter air-cooled version of the weapon as early as the 1920s. It took until the mid-1930s before the ordnance department came up with a satisfactory air-cooled version of Browning's .30-caliber machine gun suitable for infantry use. It was designated the Browning machine gun caliber .30, M1919A4, light machine gun and featured a perforated barrel-cooling jacket that brought the gun's weight down to 31 pounds. The gun was mounted on the newly designed M2 tripod that weighed only 14 pounds. The .30-caliber M1919A4 would last in army and marine service until the Vietnam War, with some being converted to fire 7.62mm ammunition.

During the Korean War, the Marine Corps had very limited numbers of the Browning M1919A6 .30-caliber light

The effort of carrying the roughly 53-pound tripod for the Browning M1917A1 .30-caliber machine gun up a steep hill is etched on the face of the marine in the foreground. For self-protection he carries an M1 carbine draped from his shoulder. The M4 bayonet that complements the carbine and its scabbard hangs from the marine's belt. The second marine trudging up the hill carries, on his shoulder, the weapon's receiver and its connected water jacket covered barrel. Real War Photos

machine gun in service. It was based on the design of the Browning M1919A4 .30-caliber light machine gun and featured a shoulder stock, a carrying handle, and a bipod mount fixed to the barrel sleeve. Other changes to the weapon intended to turn it into a cross between a light machine gun and a squad automatic weapon included a new front cover latch to allow easier opening of the receiver's cover plate and a lighter barrel with a flash hider. By doing away with the tripod of the M1919A4 the A6 version weighed only 32.5 pounds.

Besides the infantry version of the .30-caliber M1919A4 there was also a fixed version suitable for mounting in tanks as a coaxial machine gun. It was designated the caliber .30 Browning air-cooled machine gun M1919A4 fixed. An M1919A5 version was also created for use in M3 light tanks. Both wartime versions saw replacement on postwar army and marine tanks by another version designated the M37 machine gun, tank, caliber .30, fixed. Its replacement was introduced in 1959 and was designated as the machine gun, 7.62mm, M73 and fired the standard NATO 7.62mm round derived from the basic Browning design. It was not a popular weapon among U.S. tank crews, who nicknamed it the jam-o-matic.

The crew of a Marine Corps Browning M1919A4 .30-caliber machine gun awaits the appearance of Japanese soldiers before firing. The M1919A4 supposedly had a maximum effective rate of fire of between 400 and 500 rounds per minute. Like all air-cooled machine guns, the maximum useable rate of fire normally is typically no more than 150 rounds per minute to prevent the weapon's barrel from overheating and burning out. Real War Photos

.50 CALIBER MACHINE GUNS

Pictured on a firing range are marines using an M2 .50-caliber machine gun with sandbags on top of the tripod legs to steady the gun when firing. All machine gunners are taught that while they may not see enemy soldiers on many occasions, they will be directed to fire upon areas where enemy troops are suspected to be operating. This type of firing can be extremely effective in denying enemy units, the opportunity to mass troops for an attack. Defense Visual Information Center

Another machine gun that saw widespread service with the U.S. military in World War II was the recoil-operated M2 .50-caliber machine gun. John M. Browning developed the M2 in response to an army ordnance department request for a machine gun able to fire a newly developed .50-caliber (12.7mm) cartridge. John Browning had a prototype ready for testing in late 1918, but the war ended before it went into production. Browning's design for his new .50-caliber machine gun was a scaled-up version of his .30-caliber M1917 machine gun, including a water-cooled barrel.

After World War I, work continued on improving the .50-caliber cartridge as well as the Browning machine gun designed to fire it. Tests conducted by the ordnance department beginning in 1919 confirmed that both the ammunition and the gun met all the needed requirements for toughness and reliability. All the services quickly adopted the .50-caliber Model 1921. A slightly improved version of the weapon designated the M1921A1 began to appear in service by 1930. While the M1921 and the M1921A1 could be mounted on a tripod for infantry use, the guns were generally restricted to use as of antiaircraft weapons. Both versions of the M1921 disappeared from the corps inventory after World War II.

A new variant of the .50-caliber machine gun began army and marine service in the early 1930s and was officially designated as being caliber .50 Browning machine gun heavy barrel (HB) M2. It came in an air-cooled or a

A marine takes aim with a leaf-type rear sight on a Browning M2 .50-caliber machine gun. M2 gunners are taught to never forget to adjust the headspace and timing of their weapons before firing from a new barrel. Serious damage to the weapon and injury to the operator could result if these adjustments are not made. Headspace is the distance between the face of the bolt and the base of a cartridge case, fully seated in a firing chamber. Timing is the adjustment of the gun so that firing takes place when the recoiling parts are in the correct position for firing. Defense Visual Information Center

A marine installs an M2 .50-caliber machine gun on a mount in a CH-53E Super Stallion helicopter moments before the crew flew a mission to recover wounded U.S. Special Forces soldiers near Kandahar, Afghanistan in November 2001. The Marine Corps has recently tested a new, more advanced, Belgian-designed .50-caliber air-cooled machine gun for possible use on its helicopters.
Staff Sergeant Daniel C. Hottle

water-cooled configuration. The water-cooled version served as an antiaircraft gun until the end of World War II. The air-cooled version had a 45 inch barrel (early examples had a 36 inch barrel) and came configured for infantry used on a tripod or mounted on wheeled or tracked vehicles. This version of the M2 .50-caliber machine gun proved so successful that it remains in service to this day as the machine gun, caliber .50 Browning, HB Flexible. Other versions of the .50-caliber machine gun have long since been withdrawn from U.S. military service. Among them is a specially designed, postwar .50-caliber machine gun configured for mounting in the vehicle commander's cupola of M60-series tanks. It received the designation machine gun, caliber .50, fixed, M85.

Nicknamed Ma Duce or Cal Fifty, the M2 .50-caliber machine gun has a maximum effective range of 2,000 yards. Its maximum rate of fire is about 500 rounds per minute, and it weighs 82 pounds without a tripod or 126 pounds on a tripod.

Before World War II water-cooled .50-caliber machine guns were often used on navy ships as antiaircraft guns. During World War II, larger and more powerful antiaircraft guns quickly superseded them in service. The air-cooled M2 .50-caliber machine gun has now become more important to navy ships as a close-in, self-defense weapon for protection against small explosive-laden enemy vessels that may attempt to ram them in port or close to shore. Most shipboard mounts for the M2 .50-caliber machine gun feature a shield to protect the crew from small-arms fire.
Defense Visual Information Center

A marine infantryman takes aim with his M60 7.62mm machine gun. In gas-operated weapons like the M60, a portion of the expanding powder gases behind the bullet is tapped off into a gas cylinder located beneath the weapon's barrel. As a bullet travels down the barrel, gas enters the cylinder, strikes a piston, and pushes it rearward. The piston is connected by a rod to a bolt that carries the bolt with it rearward with it thereby unlocking, extracting, ejecting, and finally cocking the weapon to be able to fire the next round. Defense Visual Information Center

During World War II, the U.S. Army was impressed with the German military's M42 machine gun, which fired a 7.62mm rifle round. The M42 was reliable, rugged, and easily mass-produced. With a remarkable firing rate of over 1,000 rounds per minute, the M42 marked the debut of a new type of general-purpose machine gun (GPMG) that eliminated the need for both air-cooled light guns and water-cooled heavy guns by performing the jobs of both types of weapons. This was accomplished by reconfiguring the basic weapon with certain accessories such as a bipod or a tripod and various sighting systems.

The army quickly set out to develop its own GPMG to replace the .30-caliber M1917A1 heavy machine gun, the .30-caliber M1919A4 light machine gun, and the .30-caliber M1919A6 light machine gun. It took until 1960 before the army had a new GPMG. With the designation of a machine gun, 7.62mm M60, it was introduced at the same time as the M14 rifle and fired the same ammunition. The M60 weighed 23.2 pounds without its tripod and had a maximum rate of fire of 550 rounds per minute in theory. In practice, the weapon had a sustained rate of fire of only 100 rounds per minute. In corps service, the M60 bore the label medium machine gun and appeared in heavy weapons platoons and companies of rifle battalions.

The M60, like the German World War II MG42, was built mostly from lightweight steel stampings and pressings for ease of production. In contrast the various Browning machine guns and the BAR were machined from solid blocks of steel. Unlike the Brownings machine guns that were recoil operated, the M60 was gas operated. In this it

Introduced into Marine Corps service in time to see combat use during the Vietnam War, was the M60 7.62mm machine gun. The M60 pictured is in the hands of a lance corporal of the First Marine Division firing at Viet Cong guerrillas. The role of the M60 machine gun in corps rifle companies included supporting riflemen in the offensive and defending and engaging predetermined targets under any type of visibility conditions. Defense Visual Information Center

differed from the German MG42, which had a form of delayed blowback operation. Like the German MG42, the M60 had an integral folding bipod and provisions for mounting on tripods and various ground and air platforms.

The American designers of the M60 incorporated into their weapon a modified version of the German M42's feed

Mounted at the vehicle commander's position of a command version of an amphibious assault vehicle (AAV) is an M60D 7.62mm machine gun. It is a modified version of the standard M60 with its rear stock removed. The trigger assembly is moved from the bottom of the receiver to the rear of the weapon's receiver. To hold the weapon steady when firing, the operator gets a spade-type grip not seen in this picture. Defense Visual Information Center

Marines are pictured manning an M60E2 7.62mm machine gun. The E2 version of the M60 machine gun has a shorter barrel than the original. It also has a forward pistol grip not seen on the original. Unlike the much larger and more powerful M2 .50-caliber machine gun that needs to be head-spaced and timed every time a new barrel is fitted the headspace and timing of the M60-series machine guns are fixed. This allows the rapid changing of overheated barrels. Defense Visual Information Center

system. They also used the bolt and locking system of a German automatic rifle from World War II known as the FG-42. Despite the army's many years of research, the M60 production weapon was plagued with serious design shortcomings, such as the inability to easily change a hot barrel, since the metal carrying handle attached to the barrel would itself become extremely hot from prolonged firing. So M60 crews were given asbestos gloves to change barrels, but since the gloves often disappeared in the confusion of battle, the crews normally used rags or their uniforms to avoid being burned when changing their weapons' barrels. Another design fault discovered in field was that, in the process of disassembly and reassembly, some parts could be reinstalled backwards, making the weapon useless.

To fix the problem in the original production version, the army produced a redesigned and lightened version of the M60 designated the M60E3. However, reducing the M60E3 weight to 19.6 pounds created a serious durability problem with the weapon's receiver under sustained firing conditions. This durability problem created a great amount of dissatisfaction in the Marine Corps, which soon sought out a more reliable GPMG to replace the M60E3.

Other members of the M60 series of machine guns included the M60E2, designed for mounting in tanks as an antiaircraft gun. The M60D was designed for use as a hand-held door gun on helicopters, or mounted on the top of various wheeled or tracked vehicles. A fixed version of the M60 designed for mounting on the exterior of helicopters bore the designation M60C.

M240 MACHINE GUNS

A crewman of a Marine Corps interim fast-attack vehicle takes aim with his M240G 7.62mm machine gun. The 7.62mm ammunition fired from the weapon is very effective against exposed enemy troops. However, the effectiveness of the 7.62mm ammunition dramatically falls when confronted by enemy troops protected by intervening obstacles, such as sandbags, or the walls of buildings. For instance, at a distance of 55 yards standard 7.62mm ammunition cannot penetrate even one layer of sandbags. Michael Green

Marines from E Company, Battalion Landing Team 2/1, Fifteenth MEU are pictured assaulting an enemy position near An Nasiriyah, Iraq, during Operation Iraqi Freedom in 2003. When used in offensive operations the M240G crew may remove the weapon from its normal tripod and equip it with a shoulder sling, not seen in this picture and a bipod that is. Marines are taught to grasp the extended left leg of the weapon's bipod to help steady it when firing from the hip. It can also be fired from the shoulder. Lance Corporal Brian L. Wickliffe

To replace the unreliable and fragile M60E, the Marine Corps chose in 1994 to adopt a foreign-designed weapon by the Fabrique Nationale Manufacturing, Inc., (FN) of Belgium. Their gun fired a 7.62mm round and bears the name Mitrailleuses D'Appui General (machine gun general purpose), or more commonly the FN MAG 58. Designed in the early 1950s by M. Ernest Vervier, the FN MAG 58 incorporated some of the best features of the American Browning automatic rife (BAR) and the German MG42 machine gun. Due to its outstanding design merits, it went into service with armies around the world. In the late 1970s, the army and marine adopted the FN MAG 58 as a coaxial- and pintle-mounted machine gun for their inventory of tanks and other armored fighting vehicles. In U.S. military service this machine gun received the designation M240. It was the proven durability of the M240 mounted on marine vehicles that first attracted that service to consider adopting an infantry version of the weapon.

In Marine Corps service the infantry version of the FN MAG 58 bears the designation M240G and is classified as a medium machine gun. In army service the weapon sports the designation M240B. The marine M240G version

Right: **At Kandahar, Afghanistan, the crews of two Marine Corps M240G 7.62mm machine guns are pictured firing their weapons on a new range. Visible on top of the receivers of both weapons are the same adapter rails now mounted on the M16A4 rifles, the M4 carbine and the M4A1 CQBW. They allow the mounting of a variety of day or night optical sighting systems.** Lance Corporal Nathan E. Eason

lacks the hand-guard, hydraulic buffer, and heat shield found on the army's version making it slightly lighter. In the corps, the M240G appears in the heavy weapons platoons and companies of rifle battalions as both a defensive and an offensive weapon, but the M240G and its two-man crew are often detached to the infantry squad level when needed. Like the M60E3 it replaced, the M240G is a gas-operated, air-cooled weapon with an integral folding bipod. It can also be fired from a tripod. It weighs 24.2 pounds without the tripod and can fire up to 750 rounds per minute, although like all air-cooled GPMGs it normally fires only 100 rounds per minute under sustained fire conditions. The maximum effective range of the M240G is 1.1 miles.

Two young marines are pictured manning an M240G 7.62mm machine gun during a training exercise. Instead of mounting the weapon directly onto the tripod, the connection passes through a spring-buffered assembly on top of the tripod mount. This buffer arrangement greatly reduces the recoil shock that the gunner endures when firing the weapon. This in turn allows the gunner to more closely grip his weapon when firing and improves long-range accuracy. Michael Green

SQUAD AUTOMATIC WEAPONS

Members of the United States Marine Corps Historical Company, outfitted in reproduction World War II-era uniforms, demonstrate to the public the weapons and small-unit tactics of the era. The interpreter in the foreground is preparing to fire blanks from a .30-caliber Browning automatic rifle (BAR) during a public demonstration. Founded by Gunnery Sergeant Thomas Williams and Sergeant Timothy Kueberth, the organization's purpose is the presentation and preservation of Marine Corps history. United States Marine Corps Historical Company

Mounted on top of a Marine Corps light armored vehicle (LAV) is the D variant of the M240 family of medium machine guns. In this configuration, also seen mounted on helicopters as a door gun, the trigger assembly is moved from under the weapon's receiver to the rear of the receiver. To control the weapon's firing direction, the operator has spade grips. Greg Stewart

During World War I, the army and the marines put into service the caliber .30 Browning automatic rifle, better known to most as the BAR. It proved to be the first squad automatic weapon taken into service by the marines. Prior to time, the only automatic weapon fire available to Marine Corps infantry squads came from machine guns at the platoon or company level.

A marine armed with a .30-caliber Browning automatic rifle (BAR), takes aim with his weapon sometime during the Korean War. During that conflict, the BAR became an indispensable tool for army and marine infantrymen alike. Whenever North Korean or Chinese troops began to push through a U.S. infantry rifle line, it was fire from the BAR gunners that preserved the line. When enemy soldiers attempted to outflank forward-firing U.S. machine-gun positions, it was the BAR gunners who dealt with them. *Real War Photos*

A marine infantryman is ready to fire his M249 5.56mm squad automatic weapon (SAW) on a training range. The light machine gun fires either ball or armor-piercing ammunition. In urban combat zones, armor-piercing ammunition is not favored despite better penetration because it tends to ricochet. The ball ammunition cannot penetrate sandbags, 2-inch concrete walls, cinder blocks filled with sand, brick-veneer walls, or plate-glass windows at a 45-degree angle. It can penetrate a car body but will not normally exit the vehicle. *Hans Halberstadt*

The BAR was a gas-operated weapon with a 20-round detachable box magazine that inserted into the bottom of the weapon's receiver. It fired the same .30-06 caliber cartridge used in the various versions of the .30-caliber Browning machine guns. The BAR's original role was to provide cover to American infantry squads as they attempted to capture German defensive trenches during World War I. Combat experience with the BAR quickly showed that it was equally effective in a defensive role.

Depending on the variant, the BAR could be fired in semiautomatic or full-automatic mode. It weighed about 20 pounds with bipod, carrying handle, and loaded magazine. The weapon's maximum effective range was 500 yards.

Combat use of the BAR during World Wars I and II established its reputation as a reliable and hard-hitting demand by army as well as marine infantrymen. From 1943 through the Korean War, every four-man marine infantry fire team had a BAR. It would survive in U.S. military service until the arrival of the M14 rifle in the late 1950s.

The BAR was replaced by a modified version of the M14 rifle. It was designated the M14A1 rifle and could be fired in semiautomatic or full-automatic mode. To give the operator of the M14A1 rifle better control of the weapon in full-automatic-fire mode, it had a straight-line stock, a front-mounted folding bipod, a shoulder strap, a folding

A closeup picture of a newer-model M249 5.56mm squad automatic weapon (SAW) in the hands of a young marine wearing a protective mask. The light machine gun pictured is fitted with a red blank-firing device at the end of the muzzle. SAW sights are calibrated to a range of 1,100 yards, yet the typical SAW gunner will rarely be able to identify his targets at less than half that range. While wearing a protective mask, the gunner's ability to see and engage longer-ranged targets is limited. *Lance Corporal Robert A. Sturkie*

Lance Corporal Reyes armed with an early model M249 SAW light machine gun provides perimeter security during a rapid ground refueling of navy H-60 helicopters on November 9, 2001, during Operation Enduring Freedom in Afghanistan. Jury-rigged on a bracket above the weapon's receiver is a passive night sight. The weapon's integral rear iron sight can be seen on the rear of the weapon's receiver under the bracket.
Tech Sergeant Scott Reed

A young marine warily scans the area around his amphibious assault vehicle (AAV) with his late model M249 5.56mm squad automatic weapon (SAW) during Operation Iraqi Freedom. The SAW shown in the picture is the newest version of the weapon in use with the Marine Corps and sports an adapter rail on top of its receiver to mount a variety of day and night sights, one of which is fitted to this weapon as an example.
Sergeant Kevin R. Reed

Marine Corps infantrymen patrol a small Iraqi town during Operation Iraqi Freedom. They are armed with M16A2 rifles and an M249 5.56mm squad automatic weapon (SAW). Marine Corps rifle squads consist of 13 men, led by a squad leader with the rank of sergeant. Under his command are four fire teams of four men, each led by corporals. Each fire team is armed with a single SAW light machine gun operated by a lance corporal. Each fire team leader carries an M16-series rifle armed with a grenade launcher. The remaining two infantrymen forming a fire team are also armed with M16-series rifles, but without grenade launchers fitted. Corporal Jeff Sisto

forward handgrip, and a rear pistol grip. As the M16A1 rifle replaced the M14 rifle in army and marine service, a full-automatic version of the M16A1 took over the role of squad automatic weapon. Like the M14A1, it came with a front-mounted folding bipod to allow the soldier or marine firing the M16A1 from a prone position to steady the weapon in full- automatic mode.

Because the squad automatic weapon version of the M16A1 rifle could only fire from a limited-capacity magazine and since it did not have a changeable barrel, its ability to deliver sustained fire, like the M14A1 or BAR, on a target proved very limited. To boost firepower in army rifle squads, an effort began in 1966 to find a suitable light machine gun with the to ability to deliver sustained fire with ammunition fed to the reviver via a 200-round capacity magazine.

After much debate and testing, the army finally chose a Belgian-designed-and-built light machine gun known as the MINIMI in 1980 to fulfill the role of squad automatic weapon. The gun fires a 5.56mm round and is designated as the M249 squad automatic weapon (SAW) in U.S. military service. It first entered field use with the army in 1984 and the marines about a year later. Today one man out of every four-man fire team in the marines is armed with the SAW.

The SAW is an air-cooled, gas-operated weapon that has a quick-change barrel and may be fired from the hip, underarm, or shoulder position. A folding bipod with adjustable legs is located under the front hand guard of the weapon. The SAW has a maximum effective rate of fire of 725 rounds per minute and an effective range of 1,100 yards. The ammunition for the SAW is in a disposable molded plastic magazine that holds 200 linked rounds. With a fully loaded 200-round magazine the weapon weighs about 22 pounds. The magazine attaches to the bottom of the weapon's receiver with a dovetail fastener that has a quick-release latch. Standard M16A2 rifle 30-round box magazines can also be inserted into a magazine well on the left side of the receiver.

The U.S. military is constantly seeking ways to improve all of its weapons based on service needs and user feedback. The SAW has been through this process, making it a better weapon than when it first entered service. One of the biggest improvements to the SAW is an integral rail-mounted system mounted on top of the weapon's receiver. A variety of rail-grabber-equipped daytime optical-sighting systems or night-vision equipment can be attached to the rail system.

AUTOMATIC GRENADE LAUNCHERS

Marines pose with their Mk.19 Mod. 3 40mm automatic grenade launcher during training exercises conducted in the desert region of Southern California. The Mk. 19 is a simple recoil-operated weapon. When a round is fired, high pressure develops behind the round and forces it down a weapon's barrel. Simultaneously, this force is directed rearward to the weapon's breech and will compress springs, move levers, etc., as necessary to complete all the cycles of small-arms operation.
Michael Green

During the Vietnam War, the navy deployed a sizeable fleet of various sized boats to patrol South Vietnam's coastline as well as its interior waterways. To increase the firepower available to the crews of its patrol boats, the navy began to look for an automatic grenade launcher that could fire the same 40mm grenade as used by the single-shot M79 Grenade launcher already in use by its patrol boat crews.

The navy's first attempt at fielding an automatic grenade launcher appeared was the 19-pound Honeywell Mk. 18 Mod. 0 in 1965. Power to fire the weapon came from a hand crank, and the rate of fire was determined by how fast the weapon's gunner could turn the hand crank. Maximum effective range of the Mk. 18 topped out at 400 yards. Users of the Mk. 18 were unhappy with its performance; this led to the navy's development of the Mk. 19 40mm machine gun in 1981. The army and marines quickly perceived the Mk. 19's usefulness as a ground weapon and adopted it into service mounted either on an infantry tripod or a variety of wheeled and tracked vehicles.

Since it is a recoil-operated weapon, the Mk.19 40mm automatic grenade launcher produces a great deal of recoil shock when fired. The marine pictured is well prepared for this fact and is leaning as far back as he can to steady himself while firing the weapon. Like the M2 .50-caliber machine gun, the tripod legs on the Mk. 19 are often weighed down with sandbags to steady the weapon when firing and to prevent it from bouncing around. Defense Visual Information Center

Pictured on a table for public display is a Marine Corps Mk.19 40mm automatic grenade launcher and a few rounds of ammunition. The 40mm rounds fired from the Mk. 19 are very effective against enemy personnel in the open. In an urban environment, such as a town or city, the only material that has proven resistant to concentrated 40mm fire is dense stone such as used in some old European buildings. Michael Green

The Mk. 19 is an air-cooled, blowback-operated weapon that can fire a variety of 40mm grenades to a maximum effective range of 1,760 yards. It weighs a total of 140 pounds when mounted on a tripod. In theory, the effective rate of fire of the Mk. 19 is between 325 and 375 rounds per minute. In field use the actual sustained rate of fire is somewhere between 35 and 60 rounds per minute. The effective range of the weapon is almost 1,750 yards. Due to its weight, the Mk. 19 is not well suited for marine infantrymen on foot. It therefore tends to be restricted to mounting on vehicles.

The 40mm antipersonnel grenade fired from the Mk. 19 has an effective lethal range of 16 feet on denotation. It can also wound enemy personnel in the open within a radius of almost 50 feet. An antitank grenade fired from the Mk. 19 can penetrate almost 2 inches of steel armor. There are six Mk. 19 grenade launchers in the heavy weapons company of each marine infantry battalion. They also exist within other units in marine battalions up to regimental level.

MINIGUNS

A GAU17 7.62mm minigun has been mounted on a wooden platform overlooking a firing range to train Marine Corps helicopter door gunners. A gunner throws an arming switch to fire the weapon. This energizes the rear hand grips that mount the weapon's two triggers. One trigger starts firing the gun at 2,000 rounds per minute, pressing the second trigger increases the firing rate to 4,000 rounds per minute. Defense Visual Information Center

Air Force fighter pilots complained, during the Korean War, that the onboard M2 .50-caliber machine guns on their aircraft did not pack enough punch to knock down enemy aircraft in dogfights. To address this problem, the General Electric Company began to work on the development of a suitable air-cooled, aircraft mounted, 20mm automatic cannon. In 1956 their effort would lead to the air force introduction into Air Force service of the famous M61 Vulcan cannon.

The M61 Vulcan 20mm automatic cannon could fire up to 6,000 rounds per minute (100 shots a second) by using the same system of revolving barrels and bolts that appeared on the Gatling Gun during the Civil War. That weapon bore the name of its inventor, Dr. Richard Jordan Gatling. Modern Gatling-type guns are air-, electrical-, or hydraulic-driven.

During the Vietnam War, a need arose for a smaller version of the M61 Vulcan that could be mounted on old air force C-47 cargo planes. These twin-engine prop-driven aircraft, left over from World War II, were utilized as aerial gunships to attack North Vietnamese truck supply columns that traveled at night along the famous Ho Chi Minh Trail. Since the aircraft frame could not support

large 20mm automatic cannons and their ammunition, GE created a miniaturized air-cooled six-barrel version of the M61 Vulcan firing a 7.62mm round. The new weapon was designated the M134 or minigun. Mounted on the C-47 gunships, the miniguns were electrically powered, and their rate of fire ranged from 300 rounds per minute to 6,000 rounds per minute.

The impressive firepower of the 7.62mm minigun on the air forces' fleet of aerial gun-ships quickly resulted in the development of a ground mount-version, as well as a version configured as a door gun for transport helicopters. The corps adopted an electrically powered version as a helicopter door gun and designated it the GAU-17. In this configuration, the minigun is fed from a large ammunition box containing 4,000 rounds of 7.62mm ammunition. The entire weapon, minus the ammunition box, weighs about 35 pounds. Configured as a helicopter door gun, the minigun can fire up to 2,000 rounds per minute. To dampen the recoil and barrel torque when mounted as a helicopter door gun, the minigun is mounted on an A-frame with shock mountings.

SNIPER RIFLES

Perched on the flight-deck of a navy aircraft carrier, a marine sniper from Scout Sniper Platoon, Weapons Company, Battalion Landing Team 1/4, Thirteenth MEU, scans the area around Pier 2, Naval Station San Diego with his M40A1 sniper rifle. Snipers were part of the antiterrorism force protection exercise, which was designed to challenge marines and sailors to respond to various terrorist threats. Corporal Nathan J. Ferbert

During the early part of World War II, the marines put into service a modified version of the M1903A3 bolt-action rifle as a sniper rifle. It was designated as the U.S. rifle, caliber .30 M1903A4 (sniper). To speed up the fielding of the weapon the military acquired some commercial components including a Weaver scope. Dissatisfaction with the M1903A4 sniper rifle's performance in combat led to the fielding of another version designated as the M1903A1 sniper rifle. This version was fitted with more powerful Unertl telescope. Both versions of the M1903 sniper rifles served until the end of World War II.

The M1903A1 remained in service with the corps through the Korean War. In Korea, the marines also used sniper versions of the M1 Garand rifle designated as the M1C and M1D. During the Vietnam War, the marines used a modified version of the M14 rifle designated as the M21 sniper rifle.

By the early 1960s, the Marines got serious about fielding a dedicated sniper rifle instead of adapting an existing service rifle for the role. After much testing, the marines adopted a military-grade version of the Remington Model 700 bolt-action rifle with scope, chambered to fire a 7.65mm round. In Marine Corps service, the weapon bore the designation M40. The first batch of M40s went into use in 1966. By the mid-1970s, the M40 revealed a design weakness with the wooden stock, which resulted in the introduction of the M40A1 with a much tougher and longer-lasting fiberglass stock. It also featured a new, more powerful scope custom-built for the corps.

By the late 1990s, the corps rebuilt their existing inventory of M40A1s. The resulting changes to the M40A1 resulted in the new designation M40A3. Changes to the A3 version included the fitting of a bipod and a new stock. The most important feature on the M40A3 was the

The M40A1 pictured in the hands of a marine sniper is about 44 inches long and weighs about 15 pounds. The weapon's magazine contains five 7.62mm rounds that can reach out and touch somebody at a maximum effective range of 1,000 yards. The weapon is bedded in a commercial-grade McMillan general-purpose stock. Since 1980, the M40A1 has been equipped with a specially designed Unertl 10-power scope. Greg Stewart

In a less-than-ideal setting, a marine sniper team armed with a .50-caliber Barrett special application scoped rifle (SASR), designated the M82A1, prepares to engage any targets unfortunate enough to fall within range. The weapon's an overall length is 57 inches and weight is 30 pounds. Used as an anti-material weapon, the Barrett has proven extremely effective as a counter-sniper weapon. Greg Stewart

A close-up photograph of a Barrett special application scoped rifle (SASR) M82A1 .50-caliber sniper rifle. The SASR is normally stored in an air- and waterproof case with a pressure relief valve. The case also contains one spare 10-round magazine and cleaning equipment. The newest version of the Barrett features a lighter barrel and bolt and an improved muzzle brake. It also has an adapter rail mounted on top of the weapon's receiver to mount a variety of day and night sights. Hans Halberstadt

fitting on an accessory rail on top of the weapon's receiver that allowed mounting of an entire range of current military day and night optical sights.

A relatively recent addition to the inventory of modern marine sniper rifles is the special application scoped rifle (SASR), 12.7x99mm M82A1 that was rushed into service during the first Gulf War. It's nickname is Barrett, after the company that designed and built it. The semiautomatic, air-cooled Barrett fires the same ammunition as the M2 .50-caliber machine gun. Because of the size and power of the Barrett's ammunition, it is generally used as an anti-material weapon. It allows qualified marines to destroy enemy vehicles, aircraft, missile units, and radar units up to range of over a mile. It may also be used against enemy personnel with dreadful effect. The Barrett weighs about 37 pounds and is almost 5 feet long. It fires from a 10-round box magazine that inserts into the bottom of the weapon's receiver. The latest improvement to the Barrett is an accessory rail mounted on top of the weapon's receiver that allows many different day and night optical sights to be fitted.

ANTITANK AND ANTIAIRCRAFT WEAPONS

The M20 3.5-inch rocket launcher, nicknamed the super bazooka, consists of nothing more than a smooth-bore open metal tube, which is about 60 inches long. When loaded with a rocket, an electrical circuit exists. A magneto-type firing device in the operator's trigger grip provides the current to ignite the rocket. Once ignited, the rocket propels itself through the launcher tube by the jet action of the rocket's motor. Pictured together is a World War II, 2.36-inch, M1 bazooka and the much larger postwar, 3.5-inch, M20 super bazooka. Michael Green

Shown at the moment of firing is a Javelin antitank missile leaving its launcher container. Once the operator spots a target with the weapon's command launch unit (CLU), he places a cursor box over the image of that target. He then turns on the automatic target tracker device in the nose of the missile by transmitting a lock-on-before-launch command to the missile's electronic brain. Once the missile confirms that it is locked onto the target and ready to fire, it alerts the operator. Since the missile is self-guided to the target, the operator is free to move to another position once he fires the weapon. U.S. Marine Corps

During World War II, marine infantry units depended on a rocket launcher, known by its popular nickname as the bazooka, to protect themselves from enemy tanks. The term bazooka came from the resemblance the rocket launcher had to a strange-looking musical instrument invented by Bob Burns, a well-known radio comedian of the day. The bazooka fired a small rocket with a shape-charge (chemical-energy) warhead. Shape-charge warheads direct explosive forces in a single direction with a configuration (shape) designed to defeat a tank's armor. Most of the energy of that explosion forces itself against a target in a high-speed jet stream. This jet of hot gasses penetrates armor and causes interior destruction resulting from the heat of the gases, blast, and fragmentation of the projectile and armor.

As antitank weapons, the World War II-era bazookas, firing 2.36-inch rockets and designated the M1, had a decidedly mixed track record. In North Africa, Sicily, and Western Europe they lacked the needed penetrating power to engage and destroy heavily-armored late-war German tanks. For the marines in the Pacific theater, the threat from lightly armored Japanese tanks proved minimal. When Japanese tanks did appear in battle, the existing M1 2.36 inch bazooka easily dealt with them, and M1s were typically used against Japanese defensive positions with great success.

To overcome the M1 2.36 inch bazooka's lack of tank-killing ability, the army's ordnance department began work in October 1944 on a 3 1/2 inch bazooka that fired a much larger and more powerful rocket. Unfortunately, the new bazooka, the M20 rocket launcher, did not appear until after World War II. The M20, nicknamed the super bazooka, would serve with the marines from the Korean War to the Vietnam War. It weighed just 12 pounds and had an effective range of about 400 yards. Slightly improved models of the M20 included the M20A1 and M20A1B1 versions that functioned identically and were similar in appearance to the original M20.

The M20 rocket launcher crew consisted of three men—a gunner, an assistant gunner, and an ammunition man. In marine rifle companies, the M20 served in the antitank section of the weapons platoon. Each antitank section consisted of three squads commanded by corporals. In each squad were two weapons teams armed with M20s. Overseeing the corporals of the antitank section was a sergeant that reported in turn to the infantry company commander.

Marines undergoing training are pictured preparing themselves to fire the M72 light antitank weapon (LAW). The small 40mm grenade launched by the LAW spins in flight as a result of grooves in the barrel of the launcher. The grenades spinning causes weights in the fuse mechanism to arm the grenade after it travels a distance of about 33 yards from its launching point. The grenade then explodes on impact with its intended target.
Defense Visual Information Center

Replacing the M20 rocket launcher in the late 1960s, the Marine Corps armed itself with the shoulder-launched M72 light antitank weapon (LAW). The LAW was a self-contained one-shot, disposable, shape-charge antitank rocket launcher. The rocket inside the launcher container weighed 2.2 pounds and had a maximum effective range of 328 yards at point targets. The total weight of the LAW was only 5.22 pounds, meaning a marine infantryman could carry more than one. In the corps, the LAW was considered a light antitank weapon. The LAW was also effective against enemy defensive fortifications such as bunkers or pillboxes.

Under the right circumstances the LAW could theoretically penetrate over 11 inches of steel armor, although actual combat experience showed that it did not pack enough punch to destroy enemy tanks. To correct this design shortcoming, the army and the marines later fielded improved versions of the LAW designated the M79A1 through M79A3. The LAW saw effective use against enemy defensive fortifications such as bunkers or pillboxes.

In view of the LAW's poor armor-penetration capabilities, the corps looked for a more potent replacement. They tested many possible candidates in the late 1980s and in the end chose a Swedish-designed recoilless weapon. It fires a shape-charge antitank rocket projectile equipped with stabilizing fins. In U.S. military it is designated the AT-4 light antitank weapon, and it began army and marine service in the early 1990s. It serves in the heavy-weapons platoons of marine rifle companies.

The AT-4 is 3 1/4 feet long and weights 13.2 pounds. The antitank projectile found within the fiberglass launcher container weighs 6.6 pounds and has a maximum effective range of 500 yards. It can penetrate 15.6 inches of steel armor plate. It does not, however, pack enough of a punch to penetrate the armor of modern main battle tanks that are protected by composite armor on their frontal array. Still, the AT-4 remains a potent weapon when used to engage more lightly armored vehicles, as well as enemy defensive fortifications such as bunkers or pillboxes.

Lower Left: **A marine prepares to fire an AT-4 Light Antitank Weapon. The disposable one-piece fiberglass launch tube that contains the free-flight fin-stabilized rocket is watertight and comes fired from the right shoulder only. Deigned strictly as a close range weapon, the operator aims the AT-4 with front and rear sights, similar to those found on the M16 series rifles. For use in darkness a reusable sight bracket attaches to the weapon allowing the fitting of a variety of night vision devices.** Greg Stewart

THE SMAW

The shoulder-launched multipurpose assault weapon (SMAW) pictured has been in use with the corps since 1984 and is based on an Israeli-designed, shoulder-launched rocket system designated the B300. Its development for the Israeli military in the early 1980s reflected their need for a dual-purpose antitank and anti-fortification weapon. In Marine Corps service, the weapon is primarily used in an anti-fortification role.
Defense Visual Information Center

In the early 1980s, the marines adopted an exclusive weapon known as the shoulder-launched multipurpose assault weapon (SMAW). It is a roughly 30 pound man-portable rocket launcher that looks much like the World War II-era bazooka. While the SMAW can engage and destroy light armored vehicles, it is optimized for use against enemy defensive positions at ranges up to 275 yards.

The SMAW is more effective than the old-fashioned bazooka, because can fire an intelligent dual-mode, high-explosive, shape-charge warhead that can discriminate between hard and soft targets. On contact with a hard target such as an enemy concrete bunker the warhead detonates immediately. If an unarmored enemy truck passes into range, the warhead will detonate after penetration into the interior of the vehicle where it can do the most damage. Another 3.26 inch rocket that can be fired from the SMAW is designated as the high explosive anti-armor (HEAA) and penetrates up to 2.36 inches of armor at a maximum effective range of 547 yards.

With the old-fashioned bazooka, a loader placed the rocket round into the rear of the launcher, which was nothing more than a steel tube open at both ends. With the SMAW, a rocket round is encased in a disposable sealed canister and snaps into the rear of the 30-inch-long fiberglass launch tube. The entire weapon is 54 inches long and the sealed rocket rounds have a shelf life of 10 years.

When aiming at stationary targets, the SMAW gunner uses an optical sighting scope attached to the launcher to find his target. Once a target appears, the SMAW gunner fires a 9mm semiautomatic spotting rifle also attached to the side of the launcher. It fires a special tracer round that is matched to the flight characteristics of the rocket. If the spotting round hits the target, the SMAW gunner has a good chance of striking his intended target when he fires his weapon. For engaging moving targets such as armored cars or armored personnel carriers the SMAW gunner depends on non-optical open sights.

The operator of a shoulder-launched multipurpose assault weapon (SMAW) has just fired his weapon. When originally developed, the SMAW was intended to be used in the open, where backblast and noise from firing would not be a serious problem. The Marine Corps recently identified a need for a version of the SMAW that could be fired from enclosed spaces, like a building. Talley Defense Systems, in cooperation with the corps, developed a confined-space propulsion system for the SMAW that is now being fielded. U.S. Marine Corps

THE PREDATOR

A marine takes aim with his Predator short-range assault weapon (SRAW) at a training site. Because the weapon arms itself only 20 yards after it leaves its launcher, it's perfect for extremely close-range ambushes of enemy armored fighting vehicles in towns, cities, wooded areas, etc., that channel vehicles into areas where they cannot move about freely or use the full potential of their onboard weapons. U.S. Marine Corps

The newest light infantry antitank weapon in marine inventory is designated the Predator. It falls within the general military classification as a short-range assault weapon (SRAW). It first appeared in small numbers in the marine service in December 2003.

Like the LAW and the AT-4, the Predator is a self-contained, one-shot disposable weapon. The launch tube serves as the launch platform. The complete unit weighs less than 22 pounds and uses an arching trajectory to attack tanks at their most vulnerable point, their thin turret roof armor. The Predator's maximum effective range is 600 yards.

Once the Predator gunner has a target centered in the crosshairs of his telescopic sight, which is attached to the exterior of the missile-launch tube, he pulls a trigger and the guided missile locks onto the target. Weapons that operate like this are called fire-and-forget weapons. An inertial guidance system in the missile controls its flight profile and provides the correction commands to the four rear-mounted guidance fins. This allows the missile to follow moving targets traveling at speeds up to 22 miles per hour.

As the Predator missile approaches its intended target, the target detection device (TDD), a sophisticated electronic system in the nose of the missile, attempts to see the target with the aid of a laser range finder and a magnetic detector. Once the target is confirmed and the missile is directly over it, an explosively formed penetrator warhead is fired downward to punch a hole through the thinner armor on top of the tank's turret. The Predator is capable of defeating all known and projected armor arrays on tanks and other armored fighting vehicles.

The Predator also has a soft-launch capability that allows it to be fired from within enclosed spaces like buildings. The LAW and the AT-4 cannot be fired from within enclosed spaces because of backblast and noise. The soft-launch feature on the Predator consists of two sets of rocket propelling charges. The first charge pushes the missile out of its disposable launch tube with a minimum of recoil to a certain safe distance, at which time the second more powerful propelling charge goes off to propel the missile to its target.

The marines originally envisioned buying almost 18,000 examples of the Predator once it was ready for series production. In recent years, the marines pared back the number of Predators they wished to purchase to only 6,000 examples, but this drove up the unit cost of the weapon. As a cost-saving measure, the marines decided in October 2003 not to buy the Predator in large numbers.

Instead, the marines will retain the 730 Predator missiles and assorted training equipment acquired under a $70 million low-rate production in war-reserve status.

THE DRAGON

Due to the short range and limited effectiveness of the LAW against tanks, the army sought a more powerful shoulder-launched antitank weapon to be issued to individual infantryman. The weapon they chose in the late 1970s, which was quickly adopted by the marines, was the M47 surface-attack guided-missile system, commonly called the Dragon. It served the role of medium antitank weapon in the marines.

The Dragon was a recoilless, shoulder-fired, tube-launched, antitank weapon with a maximum effective range of 1,000 yards. It consisted of a reusable optical daylight sighting system called the tracker and a sealed missile round in a disposable launch tube. The launch tube served as the launch platform, and the tracker attached to the disposable launch tube prior to firing. The wire-guided missile fired by the Dragon weighed 15.4 pounds and had a shaped-charged warhead. Because the Dragon depended on operator guidance to the target, the operator had to keep his target in sight until impact. This would leave him vulnerable to counter fire if enemy forces identified his firing position, and the Dragon gunner had to use a separate night sight to fire at night.

Recoilless weapons deliver little recoil to their mounts or, if shoulder-fired like the Dragon, to the person firing them. The principle behind recoilless weapons is that part of the expanding gas pressure from the firing of a projectile or guided missile will counteract recoil. The main advantage of recoilless weapons over conventional guns of comparable caliber is their much lighter weight, which gives them much greater mobility. The drawback of recoilless weapons is a reduction in speed and range compared to a similar sized gun, and the tremendous blast to the rear of the weapon caused by escaping gas. The danger zone behind the Dragon when fired was 55 yards, and the backblast also alerted enemy forces to the location of the Dragon and crew.

By the 1980s, tanks had improved armor protection that greatly diminished the effectiveness of the shaped-charge warheads on the original version of the Dragon. To redress this shortcoming, the Marine Corps fielded the Dragon II, which boasted a more powerful shape-charge

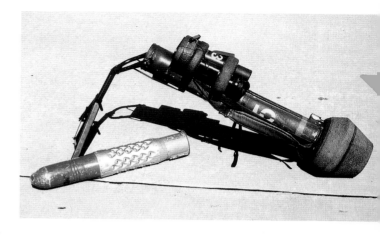

Displayed in this picture are the three major components that made up the M47 surface attack guided missile system called the Dragon. The components consist of a disposable fiberglass launch-tube container, with its integral front-mounted bipod legs; a reusable optical tracker system that attaches to the launch tube container; and the missile itself. The circular black object behind the launch tube is a removable shock absorber to prevent damage to the weapon when in transit. Defense Visual Information System

Shown at the moment of firing is a Marine Corps M47 Dragon surface Attack guided missile system. Once the missile leaves the launcher, an infrared tracking system begins to operate, and a wire link is fed out. The operator's tracker unit will compare the position of the missile (determined from the missile's infrared source on the missile) and the operator's line of sight. The tracker will send the correction commands to the missile while in flight to guide it to its target. Defense Visual Information System

warhead. This was only an interim measure until a newer generation of infantry antitank weapon could be fielded to replace the Dragon. When this happened in the late 1990s, the marines pulled the remaining Dragons from service.

THE JAVELIN

Pictured on the shoulder of a marine infantryman is the Javelin antitank missile. It replaces the Dragon antitank missile in the Marine Corps. Like the Dragon, it consists of three major components, a disposable launch container, a reusable tracker unit now called the command launch unit (CLU) that attaches to the launch container, and the missile stored within the launcher container. The circular black objects on the ground in front of the operator and mounted on the rear of the launcher container are removable shock absorbers used to prevent damage to the missile when in transit.
Lockheed Martin

Entering Marine Corps service in the late 1990s was the Javelin. Designated as a medium antitank missile, it is the replacement for the Dragon. Unlike the Dragon, which was guided in flight all the way to its target by the weapon's gunner, the Javelin is a fire-and-forget missile. Once the Javelin's gunner identifies a target in his sighting system, the intelligent imaging-infrared missile-seeker head locks onto the target and automatically guides the missile to its destination. This ability allows the Javelin's two-man crew to reload for another shot or seek cover from enemy fire immediately after firing their weapon. The Javelin has a maximum effective range of about 1 1/2 miles.

Like its predecessor the Dragon, the Javelin is a portable, shoulder-fired, tube-launched weapon. It weighs about 49 pounds in its ready-to-fire, mode and consists of a reusable command launch unit (CLU) weighing 14.1 pounds and a sealed disposable missile launch tube weighing 35 pounds. The launch tube serves as the launch platform. The CLU has a passive target acquisition and fire control unit with an integrated day sight and a thermal imaging sight for use at night or in conditions of limited visibility.

Because the Dragon was a recoilless weapon, it had a backblast problem that made it impossible to use in a confined space such as a bunker or building. The Javelin, however, has a soft-launch firing system that ejects the missile from its sealed disposable missile launch tube with a no-recoil launch. It is this soft launch that allows the Javelin to be inside a building or from other types of covered positions. Once the Javelin missile travels down range and the system verifies itself safe, the flight motor ignites, and the missile travels to its target at a high rate of speed.

Reflecting the ever-increasing sophistication of the technology that goes into modern weapon systems like the Javelin, the gunner can set the missile for different methods of attacking a target. If the intended target is a building full of enemy personnel or a hovering enemy helicopter, the gunner sets the missile seeker to hit the target head-on where it can be the most effective. If the intended target is a heavily armored tank, the gunner can set the missile to fly over the top of the vehicle and strike downward through its thinner turret roof armor. When fired at a direct-strike target, the missile travels at an altitude of about 55 feet before descending to its impact point. When set to attack a target from a steep overhead position the missile travels at an altitude of almost 500 feet before descending to its impact point.

The Javelin missile has a tandem warhead with a smaller precursor shape-charge warhead located forward of the main shape-charge warhead. The initial precursor warhead strips away any explosive reactive armor tiles found on the exterior of the tank, after which the second, much larger shape-charge warhead will pierce the underlying armor skin of the vehicle.

RECOILLESS RIFLES

Mounted on the shoulder of a U.S. soldier is the M18 57mm recoilless gun. It weighed 45 pounds and was just a little over 5 feet long. The weapon could also be mounted on a tripod. It fired either a high-explosive antitank round or a standard high-explosive round to a distance of about 4,300 yards. A few saw service with the army in World War II. The M18 entered corps service after World War II. National Archives

To supplement the bazooka in its inventory of antitank weapons, the marines adopted the recoilless rifle after World War II. Developed by the army's ordnance department during World War II, recoilless rifles came in a variety of sizes, starting with 57mm and going to 106mm. Except for the 57mm recoilless rifle, which could be fired from an operator's shoulder like a bazooka, the weight and bulk of the larger 75 to 106mm recoilless rifles mandated that they were fired from tripods or vehicle mounts.

The Marine Corps employed both the 57mm M18 recoilless rifle and the 75mm M20 recoilless rifle during the Korean War. By the Vietnam War, the corps used the 90mm M67 recoilless rifle and the M40 106mm recoilless rifle. The M40 series of 106mm recoilless rifles weighed 461 pounds on a tripod and fired a 37 pound, shape-charge, high-explosive, antitank warhead to a maximum effective range of about 8,000 yards.

Rife crews with the recoilless M40 consisted of three men: a gunner, an assistant gunner, and a loader. The weapons themselves were organized into 106mm recoilless-rifle platoons consisting of three guns with each commanded by a corporal. The platoon was in turn commanded by a sergeant who reported to the battalion commander.

The problem with larger recoilless rifles like the M40 was common to all recoilless weapons—backblast. When a 106mm projectile was fired from an M40, the backblast extended in a cone-shaped pattern up to 75 yards deep and 150 yards wide behind the weapon. This was guaranteed to attract the attention of all hostile forces within a general area and made a second shot extremely dangerous for the crew of an M40. Another problem with recoilless rifles is that the projectiles fly at such low speed that it becomes very difficult to engage and destroy moving enemy tanks at extended ranges.

Because of its weight the M40-series 106mm recoilless rifles normally went into the field mounted on a couple of different types of light, unarmored wheeled vehicles. In addition, a small three-man lightly armored vehicle was designed especially to mount six M40A1C 106mm recoilless rifles. That vehicle bore the designation multiple 106mm self-propelled rifle M50 and was nicknamed Ontos (Greek: *thing*).

Allis Chalmers built 297 examples of the Ontos for the marines between 1955 and 1957. They were rebuilt between 1963 and 1964 and were then designated M50A1. The main armament of the Ontos could be fired one at a time, in pairs, or all at once. All six of the recoilless rifles could be removed from the vehicle if needed, and two of the weapons were specifically designed for that purpose. The vehicle had a .30-caliber Browning machine gun as a secondary armament. The Ontos remained in Marine Corps service until 1980.

The smoke and dust generated by the firing of a U.S. M20 75mm recoilless rifle during the Korean War is very evident in this picture. It's not hard to understand how this might attract enemy return fire. Developed at the end of World War II, it saw only very limited use during that conflict. The M20 was used a great deal more in army and marine units during the Korean War. Because of its 114 pound weight it was normally fired from a **tripod.** National Archives

The strange-looking marine M50 Ontos antitank vehicle, armed with six 106mm recoilless rifles, weighed 9 1/2-tons and had a top speed of about 30 miles per hour. The vehicle's six recoilless weapons attached to a small pivoting fixture on the very top of the hull that allowed the guns to be elevated and traversed in unison. The recoilless rifles had a maximum traverse of 40 degrees in either direction on the front of the vehicle and a maximum elevation of up to 20 **degrees.** National Archives

Since recoilless rifles cannot be fired from enclosed spaces due to backblast, the recoilless rifles on the M50 had to be reloaded from outside the vehicle by a member of the crew as pictured. To overcome this design limitation, M50 crews tended to reload away from the direct view of enemy units if possible. The maximum effective range of the 106mm recoilless rifles was 7,515 yards when firing an antitank round. National Archives

THE TOW

To overcome the limitations of using large recoilless rifles in the long-range antitank role, the army and the marines adopted a guided missile for their next generation of infantry long-range antitank weapons. The weapon picked was the tube-launched, optically-tracked, wire-guided (TOW) missile system. It began service in the early 1970s. The army and marines consider it a heavy antitank weapon. It consists of a reusable optical sighting unit attached to a reusable launcher unit. The 3.8 foot long, 6 inch diameter TOW missiles are fired from a sealed disposable missile launch tube that fits into the launcher unit.

Mounted on a ground tripod, the entire TOW launcher unit weighs a bit over 200 pounds and is manned by a crew of five. When moved by foot, the various components break down into several pieces with none weighing more than 60 pounds. Due to its weight and size, the TOW launcher is normally mounted on a wheeled vehicle. Two different types of wire-guided antitank missiles are fired from the TOW launcher: the TOW 2A and the TOW 2B. Both weigh about 50 pounds and have tandem warheads that allow them to strip away the explosive reactive armor tiles often fitted to the exterior of tanks in service today.

Because the TOW 2A is a conventional direct-attack antitank missile, it must penetrate the thick frontal armor on tanks. Even with tandem warheads this is not always possible with newer generations of tanks with composite armor arrays designed to defeat shaped-charged warheads as mounted on antitank missiles like the TOW. To get around this problem, the TOW 2B was designed as a top-attack missile that would operate like the Javelin missile in its top-attack firing mode. The TOW 2B is now the standard version of the missle in marine corps service.

The latest versions of the TOW 2 missiles have an effective range of over 2 miles, and a well-trained crew can fire three missiles in about 90 seconds. To improve the ability of TOW crews to engage targets at longer ranges day or night, in any type of weather conditions, an upgraded launcher with a better optical system was put in army and marine service in the 1980s. It was also

A TOW 2 missile is pictured just leaving its launcher unit, mounted on the top of a Marine Corps armament carrier variant of the Humvee. Once the missile exits the launch tube, four wings unfold to provide it the ability to be steered, Steering commands to the missile in flight travel through two thin wires released from the rear o fthe missile body. As long as the operator keeps the cross hairs of his optical sighting system centered on the target with his joystick, there is a good chance of a hit. U.S. Marine Corps

A young marine recruit has just placed into the ground a practice (blue) M21 heavy antitank mine. Marine ground units use antitank minefields to hinder an attack or stop the movement of enemy armored fighting vehicles. Antitank minefields are very effective supplements to other types of antitank weapons. To be truly effective, all minefields must be anchored to natural or man-made obstacles to prevent them from being outflanked by enemy vehicles. Defense Visual Information Center

equipped with a laser range finder. Reflecting the increase in overall capabilities the improved TOW launcher system was given the designation TOW 2.

Besides killing tanks and other types of armored fighting vehicles the TOW 2 can destroy point targets such as enemy defensive positions, trucks and crew-served weapons and launchers. In the corps, the TOW 2 is used in antitank platoons of heavy-weapon companies mounted on the armament carrier version of the Humvee family of vehicles or on the antitank version of the wheeled light armored vehicle (LAV-AT). Before the introduction of the Humvee, the TOW 2 was mounted on the M151 1/4-ton light truck.

Despite its sterling combat track record with the army and marines and the continuous improvements made to its design, the TOW 2 has some disadvantages that reflect the period in which it was designed. The biggest design fault with the TOW 2 is the fact that it remains a wire-guided missile. Due to its low flight speed of less than 300 miles per hour at longer ranges it takes a TOW 2 gunner almost 17 seconds to guide a missile to a target at its maximum firing range. This makes the TOW 2 gunner very vulnerable to enemy fire or other forms of battlefield distraction that may allow his concentration to slip and lose control of the missile in flight.

Several antitank mines are now in Marine Corps service. They include the M15, the M19, and the M21. The M15 is an old-fashioned steel antitank mine a pressure plate that requires a sustained load of about 400 pounds to detonate. To prevent the 30-pound antitank mine from being removed from minefields it comes fitted with an anti-handling device that will detonate the weapon's 22-pound explosive content.

The 25-pound M19 antitank mine is predominantly plastic to make it more difficult to detect. When placed in a minefield, the M19 requires a force of 350 to 500 pounds on its pressure plate to detonate its 21-pound explosive content.

The 17 1/4-pound M21 antitank mine can mount two types of fuses, the traditional pressure plate and a thin antenna-like extension rod that projects from the ground a few inches. The M21 will detonate when it comes in contact with any part of the frontal width of a tank or other vehicle. The mine's effectiveness against armored vehicles is due to the energy produced by its 11-pound high-explosive charge when detonated which propels a mass of steel (a concave steel plate) upwards at a speed sufficient to penetrate the thin armor at the bottom of a tank's hull.

THE REDEYE

A marine is pictured placing a round of ammunition into the breech-block of an M1A1 90mm antiaircraft gun somewhere in the South Pacific during World War II. The weapon fired a 23.4-pound, high-explosive projectile to a maximum ceiling of almost 40,000 feet. The 10-man crew of the M1A1 could achieve a rate of fire of 28 rounds per minute. The combination of gun and mount weighed over 16 tons and needed a large truck to tow it from place to place. Real War Photos

During World War II, the marines depended on a variety of ground-mounted antiaircraft guns to defend itself from attack by enemy aircraft. These included the 40mm auto-

The 40mm M1 Bofors antiaircraft gun weighed a bit over 2 1/2 tons. It fired a roughly 2-pound high-explosive shell to a maximum effective ceiling of 23,622 feet. The Bofors had a maximum firing rate of 120 rounds per minute and could engage enemy aircraft to a range of 4 miles. Ammunition for the recoil-operated automatic cannon was supplied in four-round clips, as seen being with the shirtless marine in the background. Real War Photos

matic antiaircraft gun M1941, commonly called the Bofors after the Swedish company that designed it. Other important World War II marine antiaircraft guns were the 90mm M1A1 and the improved version designated the M2. It was called the triple threat because it proved extremely effective in its ability to engage not only aerial targets, but ground and sea targets as well.

In the years after World War II, as prop-driven warplanes were replaced with much faster and harder-to-hit jet-powered warplanes, antiaircraft guns were replaced with antiaircraft missiles. One of the first man-portable ground-to-air antiaircraft missiles to enter marine service was the Redeye, which became operational in 1966.

The Redeye weighed about 29 pounds in its ready-to-fire mode. It consisted of two main components, which included a reusable launcher assembly with an integral grip stock containing a battery coolant unit and a sealed disposable missile-launch tube. The missile-launch tube attached to the launcher assembly prior to a firing mission. Armed with a 4 pound, high-explosive fragmentation warhead equipped with a contact fuse, the Redeye's maximum effective range was about 2 miles to an altitude of 10,000 feet.

A marine is pictured ready to fire his shoulder-launched, Redeye antiaircraft guided missile. The missile itself came sealed inside a disposable launch tube. It did not have a proximity warhead, as do larger antiaircraft missiles. Instead, the onboard guidance system would continue to make course corrections until the last second to ensure that the missile hits its intended target. When the missile does strike an aircraft, an electrical pulse explodes the warhead.
Defense Visual Information Center

Since the Redeye had no IFF system, its operator had to confirm that an aircraft was hostile before firing. Once the operator confirmed the target, he would seek to acquire it through his optical sight and would then activate the missile's infrared seeker head. When the seeker head locked onto the hot engine exhaust of a departing enemy aircraft, it would trigger a buzzer in the operator's sight unit alerting him to fire the missile. The Redeye had soft-launch capability with a small rocket-booster charge that pushed the missile out the front of its sealed tube while the rocket motor's gases blew out the rear of the launch tube to cancel out any recoil. About 20 feet in front of the Redeye operator, the main propulsion charge would fire and push the missile to a supersonic speed of Mach 1.6 as the missile-seeker head directed itself to its intended target. The U.S. military labeled the Redeye a fire-and-forget weapon system.

THE STINGER

Because the Redeye was a first-generation, man-portable, ground-to-air antiaircraft missile, it had some design limitations. The worst of these was its inability to engage attacking enemy aircraft from the front or sides. It was strictly a tail-chase weapon, meaning that when a Redeye firing team had a chance to engage an enemy aircraft with their weapon, it had already delivered its ordnance. To overcome this design limitation, the army, along with a civilian contractor, continued to push the development of an improved version of the Redeye that could engage enemy aircraft from any direction. In military terminology this ability is known as an all-aspects target engagement capability.

mission. The passive infrared seeker head on the Stinger is more sensitive than that found on the original Redeye and can engage an enemy aircraft from any angle. The maximum effective range of the Stinger is about 5 miles to an altitude of 10,000 feet.

The Stinger boasts an integral IFF system so it doesn't have to chase the hot exhaust plume a target aircraft. An on-board guidance system known as the target adaptive guidance (TAG) will direct the missile to strike the target aircraft. To guarantee target destruction the Stinger has a 6.6 pound, high-explosive fragmentation warhead with a contact fuse. Like the Redeye, the Stinger is a fire-and-forget weapon. The two-man Stringer crew of a Stinger team can fire up to one missile every 3 to 7 seconds if needed. Fitted with a more powerful two-stage rocket motor, the Stinger's has a supersonic speed is Mach 2.2.

As with other weapon systems, the Stinger continues to be improved with the newest available technology to keep it up-to-date with current and future threats aircraft. The Stinger in corps service is mounted on a version of the Humvee called the Avenger and an air-defense variant of the corps' light armored vehicle (LAV) family of wheeled armored vehicles.

THE HAWK

A marine Corps Stinger team keeps watch for enemy aircraft during a training exercise. When a Stinger anti-aircraft missile is fired, it quickly reaches supersonic speed. The missile guides itself to its target with the aid of eight control surfaces, four in the nose section of the missile and four at the rear of the missile's body. The two-man Stinger teams normally receive warnings of approaching enemy aircraft by radio from long-range surveillance radar systems. Greg Stewart

After a prolonged period of testing to correct some technical problems that often plague cutting-edge technology, a new second-generation, man-portable, ground-to-air antiaircraft missile was placed in corps service in 1982. Instead of receiving the designation Redeye II, it was called the Stinger. It weighs 34.5 pounds and, like the original Redeye, consists of a reusable launcher assembly with an integral grip stock containing a battery coolant unit and a sealed disposable missile-launch tube. The missile-launch tube attaches to the launcher assembly prior to a firing

Aerial protection was provided for the marine ground formations against enemy aircraft for many years, and this was known as homing all-the-way killer (HAWK) antiaircraft missile system. During its early testing phase, army personnel in the Hawk program referred to it as the bullet with a brain. When originally designed in the early 1950s and fielded in the 1960s, the Basic Hawk was as a low-to-medium-altitude air-defense weapon that could travel with troops into the field. It consisted of a light, single-axle towed trailer mounting a triple launcher and several supporting units, including command and radar vehicles.

The Basic Hawk missile was 12 1/2 feet long, with a diameter of 14 inches, and a wingspan of about 4 feet. It weighed 1,295 pounds and contained a 120-pound warhead with a proximity and contact fuse. Powered by a solid-fuel rocket motor, it had a supersonic speed of Mach 2.5. The maximum effective slant range of the Basic Hawk was about 15 miles, and the missile could engage targets up to a distance of 36,000 feet.

In operation, the Basic Hawk's acquisition radar first identified an approaching enemy aircraft and relayed that

Shown during Operation Desert Storm in 1991 is a Marine Corps Hawk surface-to-air missile system. The very mobile Hawk in its final configuration was equally effective against jets and helicopters, as well as cruise missiles. It was an all-weather, day-and-night system that could continue to operate despite enemy electronic countermeasures. The Hawk system was designed to be light and mobile enough to be moved at short notice by various air force transport aircraft anywhere in the world. Defense Visual Information Center

information to the unit's illuminator radars, which painted the approaching enemy aircraft with radar waves. Some of these radar waves would reflect back to Hawk's own radar guidance system, and missile would track the enemy aircraft by following the reflected radar waves to its target.

To utilize the latest technology and remain effective against newer generations of potential enemy aircraft, an upgraded version—the Improved Hawk—was introduced in 1971. Slightly longer than the original Hawk, it could hold a larger 163-pound warhead. It also had an improved

guidance system and a new, more powerful rocket motor. The maximum effective range of the Improved Hawk increased to a slant range of 25 miles. The missile later received further upgrades under various product improvement programs (PIPs) to improve its general reliability, availability, and maintainability.

The final version of the Improved Hawk in army and marine service was the Phase III PIP. The introduction into army service in the mid-1980s of the newer and more advanced Patriot tactical air-defense missile system ended the Hawk's long career. In 1994, the active army

Fired from its two-wheeled launcher unit is a Hawk antiaircraft missile. Designed to shoot down hostile aircraft flying anywhere between 15,000 and 60,000 feet the missile carries a proximity fuse that sends out radar waves while in flight. If the radar waves bounce back after striking an aircraft, the proximity fuse will detonate the warhead within a certain distance of its target and shower it with lethal fragments. From its introduction into service in the 1960s until its final retirement from the corps in the late 1990s, U.S. armed forces never fired the Hawk in anger.
Defense Visual Information Center

began to withdraw the final version of the Hawk from service. In 1997, the last Hawk unit was deactiveatived from the Army National Guard. The marines pulled their last Hawk unit from service shortly thereafter.

INDIRECT-FIRE WEAPONS

The crew of a Marine Corps M224 60mm mortar prepares their weapon for a firing mission. It consists of a barrel, a base plate and a bipod. On the bottom of the mortar barrel, a screwed-on spherical base cap locks into a recessed socket on the base plate. The barrel of the mortar attaches to the bipod with a clamp. The bipod consists of the leg assembly, the elevating mechanism assembly, and the traversing mechanism assembly.

Defense Visual Information Center

Within the Marine Corps' inventory of indirect-fire weapons are guns, howitzers, and mortars. While the term "gun" encompasses all classes of firearms, in a strict miltary definition it is an artillery term used to describe a type of cannon. The term "cannon" is a broad term encompassing all types of artillery pieces. Artillery guns tend to have long rifled barrels and fire from towed or self-propelled mounts. Besides long barrels, guns also have high muzzle velocities and flat trajectories below 45 degrees. Artillery classified as guns generally see use for long-range, indirect-fire missions.

A howitzer is a comparatively short rifled cannon with a medium muzzle velocity fired at elevations above 45 degrees so its projectiles can reach targets protected from flat-trajectory gunfire. The howitzer's range is somewhere between that of a mortar and a gun. Compared with a gun of the same diameter bore, the howitzer fires a heavier shell at lower velocities and shorter ranges. Howitzers can be fired from towed or wheeled mounts. The distinction between artillery guns and a howitzers is now somewhat blurred due to the development of gun-howitzers that can perform both roles.

The mortar is one of the oldest and simplest forms of cannon. Mortars have short, usually smoothbore, barrels and very low muzzle velocities. By strict definition they fire projectiles at angles greater than 45 degrees, which allows them to engage short-range targets in defilade areas inaccessible to the fire of howitzers or guns.

60MM MORTARS

In certain tactical situations involving a need for lightness and quick mobility, the crew of the M224 60mm mortar may remove the standard base and replace it with a much smaller and lighter base plate, as seen in this picture. This reduction in weight and size allows one man to carry and fire the weapon. The marine in this picture shows the manner in which a 60mm mortar fires without a bipod. With his other hand he clutches a firing lever that cocks and fires a round in one movement. Michael Green

Like all major combatants in World War II, the corps made extensive use of infantry mortars. The M2 60mm was the smallest mortar, and it was based on a light mortar developed in the late 1930s by the French. In Marine Corps service, 60mm mortars provide close support to rifle companies in attack and the defense. They usually fire on small area targets such as crew-served weapons and small groups of enemy personnel in the open. On the battlefield, 60mm mortars are normally fired from the first defilade position in the rear of the frontline rifle units. Since the mortar crews in the defilade position cannot see their targets, the fire of 60mm mortars' fire is shifted and adjusted by forward observers.

The complete M2 60mm mortar mount weighed in at 45 pounds and was operated by a crew of three men. The barrel consisted of a single unit, while the mount consisted of two units, a bipod and a base plate. A sighting unit attached to the barrel. The M2's maximum rate of fire was 30 rounds for the first minute, with a sustained rate of fire of 18 rounds per minute. The maximum indirect firing range of the mortar was a bit more than 1 mile with a roughly 3-pound high-explosive round. The M2 mortar also had a direct-fire configuration when the bipod was removed and a smaller base plate was added. In this configuration, one man can operate the weapon.

Pictured firing a round is a Marine Corps M242 60mm mortar. Firing the weapon requires only that a round be inserted into the muzzle. The elevation of the barrel causes the round to slide down to the firing pin at the bottom of the barrel. The firing pin strikes the ignition cartridge at the base of the round causing a flame that ignites the powder. The gas pressure produced from the burning propellant drives the round up and out of the barrel, arming the fuse. U.S. Marine Corps

The M2 60mm mortar was in Marine Corps service until after the Korean War, when it was replaced by an improved version designated the M19 60mm mortar. By the Vietnam War, the M19 began showing its age, and the army sought a replacement. It took until 1977 before the army's efforts bore fruit with a new 60mm mortar designated the M224, which entered corps service soon thereafter. In firing order the M224 weighs 50 pounds and is operated by a three-man crew. Like the earlier 60mm mortars the M224 can be fired by one man in direct-fire without its bipod when fitted with a smaller base plate.

81MM MORTARS

During World War II the standard 81mm mortar in service with the marines was designated the M1. Like the M2 60mm mortar, the M1 81mm mortar was based on a French-designed mortar from the late 1930s. Like all 60mm and 81mm mortars, it consisted of three major separate components that broke down for ease of transport. They included the barrel, the bipod, and the base plate. All mortars come fitted with a sight that attaches to its yoke.

The sight consisted of a collimator, an elevation and deflection mechanism, and longitudinal and cross-levels. It allowed the mortar crew to lay (aim) in their weapon in both elevation and direction.

In the Marine Corps, 81mm mortars are used at the battalion level. Their purpose is to provide supporting fire to rifle battalions in attack or defense. The 81mm mortar is an excellent weapon for firing on area targets, such as troops in the open and enemy assembly areas. Since mortar crews cannot see their targets, the fire of the 81mm mortars is shifted and adjusted by forward observers who can see the targets. Battalion-level 81mm mortars are usually fired in unison to maximize their battlefield effectiveness. Firing control for the 81mm mortars comes from a fire direction center, which computes firing data for the mortars.

In firing order the complete M1 81mm mortar weighed 136 pounds. The maximum effective rate of fire for the M1 was 35 rounds for the first minute, and 18

A crewman from a Marine Corps M1 81mm mortar crew is pictured cleaning the barrel of his weapon somewhere in the South Pacific during World War II. Another member of the crew is holding an 81mm mortar round on his bare shoulder to prepare to restart the firing mission. The M1 could fire three different types of high-explosive rounds. The heaviest was the 15.1-pound M56. Due to its weight the M1 could only propel the M56 to a maximum range of 1,300 yards. Real War Photos

The place is South Vietnam. The date is September 1, 1968. Marines of the Third Division prepare to fire their M29A1 81mm mortar to suppress North Vietnamese mortar fire while a marine transport helicopter drops into a nearby landing zone. Like most infantry support mortars the firing positions are in close proximity to each other, yet are far enough apart to avoid damage to more than one mortar by the burst of a single shell. U.S. Marine Corps

Pictured in the field during a training exercise is an unattended Marine Corps M252 81mm mortar with a blast-attenuation device (BAD) affixed to the muzzle end of the barrel. Besides reducing the effects of noise and concussion from blast overpressure on the crew every time a round is fired, the BAD also helps to reduce the weapon's muzzle flash, making it harder for enemy observers to identify the mortar's firing position. Michael Green

The crew of a Marine Corps M252 81mm mortar prepares a high-explosive round for firing. Mortar rounds for the M252 bear the designation semi-fixed, complete ammunition. It's semi-fixed since the propelling charge is in increments and is adjusted to vary the range of each round like artillery ammunition. It's complete since each round comes packed in an individual container with fuse and propelling charge attached. U.S.Marine Corps

rounds per minute sustained rate of fire. The maximum effective range of the M1 mortar was slightly less than 2 miles with a 6.87-pound high explosive projectile. The M1 mortar remained in corps service until it was replaced in the 1960s by the M29 81mm mortar. In firing order, the complete M29 weighed 115 pounds and had a maximum effective range of almost 3 miles. The rate of fire for the M1 and the M29 were roughly comparable. A slightly improved version of the M29 mortar designated the M29A1 appeared later.

The army began to look for a replacement for the M29A1 81mm mortar in the mid-1970s. They needed a mortar that could fire a new generation of more powerful mortar ammunition in development at the time. These new mortar rounds created much higher chamber pressure in mortar barrels than the existing mortar ammunition, but in exchange offered longer ranges and more potent rounds. The most promising candidate to meet the army's needs was a British-designed mortar designated the 81mm L16ML. It was introduced into British army service in the 1970s. In an agreement with the British government, the U.S. Army had the British builder adapt their mortar for U.S. military use. In U.S. military service, the new 81mm was designated the M252. It entered marine service in 1986. Marines refer to the M252 simply as the 81. It fires high-explosive, white and red phosphorus along with illumination round. The M889 high-explosive round weighs 9.4 pounds and has a burst radius of almost 50 yards. There are eight M252s in the mortar platoon of each marine infantry battalion. To reduce the blast effect on the crew a blast attenuation device (BAD) is attached to the muzzle of the M252.

4.2-INCH M30 MORTARS

Another World War II mortar used by the Marine Corps into the postwar era was the 4.2 inch (107mm) M30 mortar, nicknamed the four-deuce. It was originally developed by the army's chemical corps to fire poison gas or smoke projectiles. The development of a suitable high-explosive shell for the weapon led to its use in support of infantry units. In this role, the weapon's accuracy, high rate of fire, and terrific shock action impressed all who sought its support in combat.

The M30 mortar fired a 27-pound high explosive projectile out to a range of 3 miles. It took an eight-man crew to service the weapon. In combat, firing of the M30

A U.S. soldier is pictured preparing to drop a round down the muzzle of a very impressive looking 4.2-inch 117mm) mortar. The weapon in army and marine service was designated the M30. Unlike the 60mm and 81mm mortars that have smooth-bore barrels. The M30 barrel was rifled, which imparted spin to the round as it left the barrel to help stabilize it in flight. The smaller 60mm and 81mm mortar rounds have fins to stabilize them in flight. Defense Visual Information Center

An impressive plume of flame marks the firing of a round from a French-designed-and-built 120mm rifled mortar under going testing by the Marine Corps in 2002. The semiautomatic, breech-loaded weapon is designated the 2R2M and is pictured mounted on a French-army version of the light armored vehicle (LAV) used by the corps. The marines also conducted test with a towed version of the weapon. Sergeant Ken Griffin

came under the control of a fire-direction center and was adjusted by forward observers.

The M30 had some disadvantages; the biggest of which was its 650-pound weight in firing order. While the mortar broke down into six major components—barrel, base plate, base ring, bridge, rotator, and standard—the weight of the individual components dictated that it could be hand carried only short distances. This tended to restrict the M30 to static roles. The M30 was removed from Marine Corps service following the Vietnam War.

Only recently has the Marine Corps begun reexploring the possibly of fielding a new heavy mortar. Instead of another 107mm mortar, the corps is now interested in a larger 120mm mortar. The army already has a 120mm mortar in service, and the 120mm is now a standard in armed forces throughout the world. The Marine Corps has already begun testing different types of 120mm mortars.

TOWED HOWITZERS AND GUNS

A crew of a Marine Corps M1A1 75mm pack howitzer prepares to fire on Japanese positions during World War II. The first version of the howitzer entered army service in 1927. To keep the weight down to an acceptable level, the weapon was fitted with a lightweight perforated box trail. Early versions had wood-spoked wheels. The howitzer pictured has pneumatic tires. Real War Photos

One of the smallest towed howitzers in use by the Marine Corps in World War II was the 75mm Pack Howitzer M1A1. The 1,500-pound weapon fired a 17-pound high explosive round out to a range of about 5 miles. The 75mm

The crew of a Marine Corps M101A1 105mm howitzer has just fired at enemy positions during the Korean War. The gun carriage is a two-wheel, split-trail-type and has an armored shield to protect the gun crew. For towing, the two separate sections that form the split-trail lock together. When set up for a firing mission the split trails spread out as far as possible (as seen in this picture) to help absorb recoil, stabilize the howitzer, and keep it from moving when fired. Defense Visual Information Center

pack howitzer disappeared from corps service by the end of 1945 and was replaced by a 105mm towed howitzer.

The towed 105mm howitzer M2A1 was the mainstay of the marine howitzer inventory in World War II. First introduced into U.S. military service in 1940, the M2A1 remained in production until the early 1950s, with over 10,000 units built. It weighed about 2 tons and was classified as a light artillery piece. The main mission of light artillery pieces was antipersonnel in nature, particularly against troops in the open. It took an eight-man crew to service the weapon.

The maximum rate of fire of the M2A1 was 10 rounds per minute for the first three minutes, with a sustained rate of fire of three rounds per minute. The maximum effective range with the M2A1 firing a 33-pound high explosive round was almost 7 miles. After World War II, the M2A1 was redesignated the M101, and later an improved model was designated the M101A1. The

A young marine is sorting through various 105mm projectiles for his M101A1 105mm howitzer. Most artillery projectiles have the same general shape; a cylindrical body, a sharply pointed head, and a fuse at the very tip of the projectile. An artillery fuse causes a projectile to explode where and when it's needed. Defense Visual Information Center

The barrel of a Marine Corps M101A1 105mm howitzer in full recoil at the moment of firing. Because the recoiling barrel is completely horizontal, the weapon is firing at a target in direct view of the gun crew. This is not standard practice with artillery pieces in the U.S. military except for special situations, since this tends to leave a very valuable asset vulnerable to enemy direct fire. Defense Visual Information Center

Pictured during World War II is a Marine Corps M3A1 half-track armed with a 75mm gun designated the M1897A4. Armed marine hitchhikers sit on the front of the vehicle. The forward-firing 75mm main gun had a traverse rate of only 42 degrees (21 degrees right and 21 degrees left). The maximum elevation of the gun in this picture was 29 degrees. The maximum depression of the gun was restricted to less than 7 degrees. Storage space was available onboard the vehicle for 56 of the 75mm main gun rounds. Real War Photos

M101A1 continued in field use with marine artillery battalions until the early 1990s, and some remain in the inventory today as ceremonial weapons only.

Another World War II artillery veteran that the Marine Corps used in the postwar years was the M1 155mm towed howitzer. More than 6,000 M1s came off U.S. production lines for use by the marine and army during World War II. They remained in marine service until the early 1980s. After World War II, they were redesignated as the M114 155mm towed howitzer. Improved models of the weapon were designated as the M114A1 and M114A2. In marine service, the 155mm howitzer acquired the nickname the Pig due to its size and weight. The Pig weighed in more than 6 tons and was serviced by a detachment of 11 men.

The range of the M114 95-pound high-explosive round was about 9 miles. When firing a rocket-assisted round, the M114 could reach targets over 12 miles away. The weapon had a maximum rate of fire of 10 rounds for the first minute. Its sustained rate of fire was about three rounds per minute. Classified as a medium artillery piece, the weapon was intended for engaging enemy artillery, dug-in enemy personnel, and soft-skin vehicles.

Before World War II, the marines used the M1897A2 gun, better known as the French 75, as its standard light artillery gun. It fired a 12-pound high-explosive round to a maximum range of 4 miles. The replacement for the French 75 at the beginning stages of World War II was the 75mm Pack Howitzer M1A1. Later in the war, the marines placed into service the 155mm gun M1A1, better known as the Long Tom. This roughly 5-ton weapon could fire a 95-pound high-explosive round to a range of 14 miles. The rate of fire for the Long Tom proved to be only one round per minute. The Long Tom remained in corps service through the Korean War.

SELF-PROPELLED ARTILLERY

Besides towed artillery, the marines made use of self-propelled artillery from World War II until the early 1990s, with the French 75 being one of the first since it was mounted on a half-track. While originally designed by the army for use as a mobile antitank gun, in marine service, the vehicle, classified as the M3 or M3A1 75mm gun motor carriage, was used as an assault gun in attacking Japanese bunkers or in a standard indirect artillery-fire role. The marines retired the M3 by the end of World War

An M53 155mm self-propelled gun is pictured operating with the Second Marine Division in Puerto Rico during a training exercise in 1953. The M53 was based on various components of the medium tanks M47 and M48. Unlike postwar U.S. tanks that had rear-hull-mounted engines and transmissions, the M53's engine and transmission were at the front of its hull, leaving the rear of the chassis free for mounting the turret, which carried a 155mm gun. National Archives

The counterpart to the M53 155mm self-propelling gun in Marine Corps service was the M55 8-inch (203mm) self-propelled howitzer. The range of the 203mm gun was a bit less than the 155mm gun, but it made up for that by being more accurate than the 155mm gun. Both guns were interchangeable between vehicles. National Archives

The Marine Corps M109A3 155mm self-propelled howitzer pictured is taking part in a field-training exercise. The crew has covered the projectiles stacked behind the vehicle with tarps to keep them from overheating. Crewed by six men, a vehicle commander, a gunner, a driver, and three ammunition handlers, the M109 hull and turret were built from thin welded aluminum armor that offered protection only from some types of small-arms fire and artillery fragments. Greg Stewart

The M110A2 8-inch (203mm) self-propelled howitzer pictured once formed an important part of the Marine Corps' arsenal of artillery weapons. The howitzer was designed to be elevated up to 65 degrees and traversed 30 degrees either left or right from the centerline of the vehicle. It fired separate loading ammunition in contrast to the semi-fixed ammunition used in the M101A1 105mm howitzer. This meant that the projectile, propelling charge, and primer came loaded in the breech of the howitzer separately. Greg Stewart

II, and its replacement was the full-tracked M7 Priest that mounted the M2A1 105mm howitzer in an open-topped compartment. The Priest began corps service in 1945 and was retired at the end of the Korean War.

In the years following World War II, the army development of a line of specialized self-propelled vehicles able to mount a variety of guns and howitzers. Not all of were adopted by the Marine Corps. Beginning in the late 1950s, the corps did adopt the M53 and M55. Both vehicles were identical except for the weapon they carried. The M53 mounted the 155mm Long Tom gun, while the M55 mounted an 8-inch howitzer. The M53 and M55's weapons were installed in a fully enclosed armored turret that could traverse an arc of 60 degrees across the front of the vehicles. The M53 and M55 lasted in marine service until the Vietnam War.

It was during the Vietnam War that the Marine Corps put into service the first version of the M109 series of self-propelled 155mm howitzers. The armored turret on the M109 series of vehicles could be traversed 360 degrees, unlike turrets on the M53 and M55. Between the 1970s through the 1980s, the army progressively improved the M109 series, which created many different versions of the vehicle appearing in army and marine service. They included the M109A1, followed by the M109A2, and the M109A3, and finally the M109A4. The marines retired their inventory of M109 series vehicles in the early 1990s in favor of its towed 155mm howitzers.

Besides the specialized, armored, full-tracked self-propelled artillery pieces developed by the army and adopted by the marines, the army had also developed, in the early 1960s, a lightly armored chassis that could mount either a very-long-barreled 175mm gun or an 8-inch howitzer. With the 175mm gun, the vehicle was known as the M107; when fitted with the 8-inch howitzer, it was known as the M110. To keep the vehicles' weight down so it could be air-transportable the weapons were installed on an exposed rotating platform on the rear of the vehicle's chassis. The mounted the weapons could be traverse 30 degrees left or right to the front of the vehicles. The marines used both the M107 and M110 during the Vietnam War. Subsequent improvements to the vehicles and their weapons resulted in an A1 version of the M107 and an A1 and A2 version of the M110. Neither vehicle remains in corps service, and the M110A2 ended service in early 1990s.

The crew of a Marine Corps M198 155mm towed howitzer is pictured preparing their weapon for firing. The marine in the foreground digs in the spade mounted on one of the weapon's two split-trail legs. A spade is a bearing surface that is usually found on the back end of the trails of an artillery carriage that's dug into the ground to restrict movement of the weapon during recoil. *Defense Visual Information Center*

Pictured is an M939 5-ton truck pulling an M198 155mm towed howitzer through a swamp. Development of the weapon began under the army's stewardship in 1968. By 1970, an advance developmental prototype underwent firing tests. Positive feedback on early firing trials led to an order for two prototypes that were delivered to the army in 1972. Eight more howitzer prototypes soon followed. Prototype testing confirmed that the howitzer met of all the army's requirements, and production began at Rock Island Arsenal in 1978. *AM General*

The eventual replacement for the 105mm towed M101A1 and the 155mm towed M114 in Marine Corps service was the M198 155mm towed howitzer. Marine Corps artillery men called the weapon the niner-eight. Beginning marine service in 1982, the M198's most important feature at that time was its 18-mile maximum effective range with a rocket-assisted projectile. Firing a conventional 95-pound artillery projectile, the M198 could reach a distance of 14 miles. In addition to its increased range, the M198 was specifically designed to use all stockpiled 155mm howitzer ammunition, as well as new projectiles and propelling charges in development.

In the field, the M198's nine-man crew can ready the weapon for firing in less than 6 minutes. Once in firing position, the wheels of the M198 are lifted hydraulically about 7 inches above the ground, bringing the carriage to rest on its firing base (a circular aluminum structure suspended under the lower carriage). The M198 has a two-piece carriage (a carriage or mount is an assembly that furnishes a support for a weapon in firing or traveling order) with the top carriage carrying the barrel, the elevat-

The loaders for an M198 155mm towed howitzer await the call for the next fire mission. Because the 155mm projectiles weigh up to 100 pounds each, the loaders lay them onto a loading tray as seen in this picture. The marine directly behind the 155mm projectile on the loading tray holds a long metal rammer staff. Once the loading tray aligns with the open breech of the weapon, the rammer shoves the projectile into the barrel of the weapon. *Michael Green*

In this picture, the two loaders seen in the preceding photograph are racing to the open breech of their weapon with their hand-carried loading tray. Behind the loading tray, the head of the rammer staff is visible. Standing to the left of the loaders is the powder man holding a powder charge, which goes into the breech behind the projectile. Michael Green

This picture captures the moment at which the two loaders of a 155mm howitzer are trying to get their loading tray out of the way of the marine who is shoving the 155mm projectile into the rifling of the barrel with his rammer staff. The rifled grooves inside the weapon's barrel hold the projectile tightly in position. The marine on the right is inspecting the weapon's panoramic telescope used for laying the weapon during indirect fire missions. Sergeant Brian J. Griffin

ing mechanism, and the equilibrator. (An equilibrator is a device that overcomes the unbalanced weight of the barrel in its carriage and keeps the weapon in balance at all angles of elevation when elevated or depressed.)

The M198 has a maximum effective rate of fire of four rounds per minute for the first 2 minutes and a sustained rate of fire of two rounds per minute. A thermal sensing device on the barrel of the M198 warns the gun crew when the tube becomes too hot to fire safely. A hydro-pneumatic variable-length recoil system allows a maximum recoil length of almost 6 feet when the weapon is firing its most powerful propelling charge. The hydro-pneumatic recoil system uses the force of compressed gas to return a barrel from its recoiled position to its in-battery position.

A recoil system is a mechanism designed to absorb the energy of recoil gradually and to avoid violent movement of the weapon carriage. It normally consists of three components: a recoil brake to control recoil and limit its length, a counter-recoil mechanism to return the recoiling parts to their firing position, and a counter-recoil buffer to diminish the shock of the recoiling parts returning to firing position.

The M198 is not a small weapon. In its towed configuration, it's 40 feet 6 inches long, 9 feet 2 inches wide, and 9 feet 6 inches tall. While the weapon is air-transportable by C-130 Hercules transport planes, only the corps' largest and most powerful helicopter, the CH-53E Super Stallion, can lift the 8-ton M198.

Because the M198 does not have a suspension system, there has been a continuing series of problems with excessive wear on the carriage. A host of other maintenance problems has also plagued the M198 since its introduction into service. The original towing vehicle for the M198 was the M813 5-ton truck, which proved to have serious problems moving the weapon in certain types of terrain. To overcome this problem, the M813 5-ton truck was replaced, in 2003, as a towing vehicle for the M198 by the larger and more powerful medium vehicle tactical (MVTR) 7-ton truck.

M777 LIGHTWEIGHT 155MM HOWITZER

Dissatisfaction with the weight of the M198's weight many maintenance problems was not just a Marine Corps concern. The army's inventory of M198s had the same problems. A decision by the army's top brass in the mid-

1980s led to a search for a slimmed-down 155mm towed howitzer with better durability than the M198.

A possible replacement candidate for the M198 in army service was a design proposed by the Armaments Division of Vickers Shipbuilding and Engineering Limited (VSEL). Vickers had conceived the idea for a very lightweight, towed, 155mm howitzer that if built, would weigh half as much as existing NATO standard 39 caliber 155mm towed howitzers. Vickers' armaments division later became BAE SYSTEMS RO Defense.

VSEL approached the U.S. Army and offered to build a prototype howitzer at company expense if the army would evaluate the weapon. The army quickly confirmed its interest and VSEL completed two prototypes in 1989. VSEL referred to them as the 155mm ultra-lightweight field howitzer (UFH). The corps also began to show a keen interest in the weapon. Because of this, testing of one of the two prototypes of the UFH began in the United States in 1990 on behalf of the Marine Corps. The corps soon picked the UFH for further development after a competitive shoot-off with other contenders in 1997. Eight engineering and manufacturing development (EMD) howitzers soon followed. They underwent a series of grueling tests over a 5-year period. The U.S. military designated these pre-production weapons as the XM777. They also became known as the XM777 lightweight 155 howitzer (LW155).

The next step with the XM777 involved BAE SYSTEMS RO Defense, transferring the manufacturing technology to the United States. Two pilot production howitzers were soon introduced in 2002, using the U.S. supplier base. Testing of the pilot production XM777s convinced the U.S. Department of Defense (DOD) of the weapon's suitability for service. In November 2002, DOD approved a low-rate initial production of 94 examples of the XM777 for the corps, at a total cost of $135 million dollars. The Marine Corps will begin fielding the first M777s in 2005. Once in series production, the letter X will be removed, and the weapon's designation will be the M777. As more funding becomes available, the USMC plans on adding 283 more examples of the M777 to its order with BAE Systems. The army will acquire at least 233 M777s.

The M777 is 25 percent smaller than the M198 that it's replacing, and it will come manned by a crew of nine, although a reduced crew of five can still operate the weapon if needed. The general operational parameters of the M777 are roughly comparable to the M198 with rocket-

Visible in this dramatic picture is the method by which the large muzzle brake mounted at the end of the M198 155mm towed howitzer barrel helps reduce recoil and dissipate the gaseous energy created when firing. The baffles of the muzzle brake deflect powder gases slightly backward of the howitzer muzzle to the outside atmosphere producing a forward force on the muzzle brake, thus serving to reduce recoil action. Defense Visual Information Center

A picture from the first Gulf War shows a Marine Corps M198 155mm towed howitzer firing at Iraqi military targets. The M198 can fire a wide assortment of special-purpose projectiles, including those containing antitank and antipersonnel mines or grenades, which are designed to discharge from the projectile over a target area and either fall to the ground to explode on impact or guide themselves to targets by various methods. Defense Visual Information Center

Taken during Operation Iraqi Freedom is this picture showing a gunner on a Marine Corps M198 155mm towed howitzer who has just pulled on the lanyard that connects to a firing mechanism that fires the weapon. With a maximum powder charge, the barrel of the M198 will recoil as much as 6 feet, which seems to be the case in this picture. U.S. Marine Corps

Shown in firing order is a prototype XM777 lightweight 155mm howitzer. Like the M198 155mm towed howitzer, it has a split-trail arrangement at the rear of the weapon's carriage. To help stabilize the M777 in firing order, it sits on a firing base with its wheels in a raised position like the M198. Unlike any other U.S. artillery pieces the M777 has two smaller trail legs that extend out the front of the carriage when firing to stabilize the weapon. BAE SYSTEMS RO Defense

assisted projectiles and conventional artillery projectiles. The maximum rate of fire of the M777 is the same as the M198. In contrast to the 8 tons of the M198, the M777 weighs less than 5 tons. This difference in weight with the M777 can be attributed to making most of the weapon carriage from advanced materials like titanium, which significantly reduced weight while maintaining the strength and durability of the weapon's carriage.

The reduced weight of the M777 compared to the M198 means that its off-road mobility is far superior. Unlike the M198 that now calls for a 6x6 heavy truck to tow it around, the M777 is light enough to be towed by smaller vehicles. The riding performance of the British-designed howitzer is far superior to the M198 since it comes fitted with a hydro-strut suspension system. The reduced weight of the M777 also means that it can be airlifted by a greater variety of helicopters in both marine and army service. It can also be airlifted by the Marine Corps' new V-22 Osprey tilt-rotor aircraft and tests conducted in 1999 showed that the howitzer is indeed compatible with the Osprey. The corps anticipates that the Osprey will carry the M777 from either ship or land-based positions to forward locations to support marines on future battlefields.

To improve the firing accuracy and reaction time of the M777, General Dynamics Armaments and Technical Products, under contract to BAE SYSTEMS, is developing a towed artillery digitization (TAD) system for the weapon. This fire-control system will attach to individual M777s and offer crews digital communications with the advanced field artillery tactical data system (AFATDS), giving them navigation, pointing and self-location information. Current plans call for the TAD system to be fielded by 2006. M777s equipped with the TAD will have the designation M777A1. Planned software improvements to the TAD will lead to the eventual designation of a M777A2 version.

ROCKET SYSTEMS

Late in World War II, the Marine Corps began to deploy a small number of self-propelled rocket detachments equipped with light trucks, on which were mounted various configurations of multiple-tube rocket launchers. These rocket-equipped trucks first saw use with the corps during the capture of the Japanese-held island of Saipan in June 1944. They would continue to see service through the end of the war in the Pacific. By the time the

marine invaded the heavily-defended island of Iwo Jima in February 1945, their standard self-propelled rocket launcher consisted of a 25-rail launcher placed on the rear cargo bay of an International Harvester 1/2-ton 4x4 truck model M-1-4. During the fighting for Iwo Jima, the marine rocket truck crews fired over 14,000 rockets.

The standard rocket used by the corps during World War II for its self-propelled rocket launchers was designated the M8. It was 33 inches long, had a diameter of 4 1/2 inches and weighed a little over 8 pounds. The M8 warhead contained 4.3 pounds of high explosive. The maximum range of the rocket topped out at 4,600 yards. Accuracy of the rocket was poor and proved to be a constant problem. Another problem involved the large amount of flame and smoke generated when the rockets were fired. This visual signature quickly resulted in enemy counter-battery fire that taught the marine crews the importance of moving as fast as possible to a new firing location once a firing mission had been completed. In

Pictured in use in late World War II is a firing line of Marine Corps International Harvester 1/2-ton, 4x4, model M-1-4 light trucks converted to multiple rocket-launcher vehicles. Powered by a six-cylinder, 85-horsepower, gasoline engine, the vehicle saw service only with the marines and the navy. An ambulance version of the vehicle also served in World War II. Real War Photos

modern military terminology this practice is known as shoot-and-scoot. Despite these disadvantages, no other weapon system could put as many high-explosive rounds into an area as fast as multiple rocket launchers.

Shortly after World War II, the Marine Corps disbanded its truck-mounted, self-propelled rocket

detachments. In their place, the corps formed new rocket detachments equipped with an army-developed, towed, two-wheel trailer mounting a 24-rail rocket launcher designated the T66. Instead of the World War II-era 4 1/2-inch M8 rocket, the T66 fired an improved version, designated the M16 that offered increased in range and accuracy over the M8. The T66 was later became known as the M21 in corps service.

The M21 would remain in use with the marines up through the Korean War. Since that time, the corps has gone without any type of multiple rocket launcher system. The marines began to rethink that situation in 1998 when the army acquired four prototype versions of a new self-propelled rocket launcher called the high mobility artillery rocket system (HIMARS). Developed by Lockheed Martin Missiles and Fire Control Division, the HIMARS consisted of a six-tube rocket launcher, mounted on the rear cargo deck of a 5-ton 6x6 truck.

In 2001, the army procured an additional six HIMARS to test purposes. At this point, the Marine Corps procured

Taken during the Korean War, this picture shows a Marine Corps M21 multiple towed rocket launcher at the moment of firing. Most of the weapon's crew is trying to plug their ears to muffle the terrible noise generated by firing the large rockets. For firing the M21, the carriage is emplaced with the trails spread in the same manner as a conventional artillery piece, and a firing pedestal is lowered to the ground. Real War Photos

from Lockheed two HIMARS to be delivered at the same time as the army's examples. Lockheed delivered the vehicles to the army and marines in 2002. Marine Corps testing of the HIMARS will continue until 2004 to determine if the weapon systems will prove suitable for its needs.

The 227mm unguided rockets fired from the launcher on the HIMARS vehicle are designated the M26. Each

rocket is about 13 feet long and weighs 676 pounds. As are all rockets, the M26 is a dumb round. Flight trajectory is dependent on launcher-tube elevation at firing time. The M26's range is about 20 miles, while a new, guided, extended-range rocket can reach a distance of almost 37 miles. The HIMARS configuration can also be changed to fire a single army tactical missile system (ATACMS). This large, 13-foot-long guided missile can reach ranges up to 186 miles.

The impressive firepower of the high mobility artillery rocket system (HIMARS) is clearly evident in this picture taken at Marine Corps Base Camp Lejeune, North Carolina, on July 28, 2000. The corps is now testing the suitability of the weapon system for incorporation into its arsenal of artillery weapons. Since it's much smaller and lighter than the M198 155mm towed howitzer the HIMARS will make better use of existing navy and air force transportation assets.
U.S. Marine Corps

WHEELED WEAPON-EQUIPPED VEHICLES

The open-topped, four-wheel-drive M3A1 scout car used briefly by the Marine Corps during World War II weighed in at 4 tons. Armor protection was limited to a 1/4-inch armor plate except on the front armored windshield which had 1/2-inch plate. The vehicle's normal armament was three machine guns mounted on a skate rail that encircled the interior of the vehicle. The M3A1 pictured belongs to the Military Vehicle Technology Foundation (MVTF) and bears pre-World War II army markings. Michael Green

During World War I, the Marine Corps first took an interest in wheeled armored fighting vehicles. In 1916, the corps acquired for testing an armored car built by the Armored Motor Car Company (AMC). The vehicle was called the King armored car since it was based on the modified chassis of a King Motor Car Company touring car (with the addition of rear dual wheels). The three-man vehicle had a turret-mounted .30 caliber machine gun and was powered by an eight-cylinder gasoline engine.

Above: **A Marine Corps light armored vehicle-25 (LAV-25) pauses for a moment near some bushes during training. Armor protection on the vehicle will only defeat some types of small-arms fire and artillery fragments. Visible just behind the rear tire is one of the vehicle's two sets of combination propellers and rudders that both power and steer the LAV-25 in the water.** Michael Green

The marines must have liked what they saw, because they soon acquired seven more King armored cars from AMC. While the King armored cars did not see service during World War I, they were used as internal security vehicles by the marines in Haiti in 1920s. It was during this period that the corps began to focus its limited resources on light tank development and away from armored cars. In 1934 the King armored cars passed out of service.

In the late 1920s, the Marine Corps acquired a single White Model 15-B armored car. It might have been considered as a possible replacement for the aging King armored cars. Funding shortfalls effectively ended the project before any additional White armored cars could be bought.

During World War II, the corps put into service a small number of open-topped, lightly armored, M3A1 scout cars armed with both .30-caliber and .50-caliber machine guns. These 4 ton 4x4 vehicles were built by White Motor and served briefly before being phased out of service by 1943. The corps would not put in service another wheeled armored fighting vehicle until the early 1980s.

A series of dramatic events in 1979 caused the U.S. military establishment to rethink its procurement policies regarding wheeled versus tracked armored fighting vehicles. The first of these events was the overthrow of the pro-U.S. leader of Iran by an Islamic radical movement in February 1979. In November, Iranian students seized the U.S. Embassy and its staff in Iran, and in December the Soviet military invaded Afghanistan.

Because the bulk of U.S. ground military power was designed to stop a possible Soviet invasion of Western Europe, it was not suited to respond quickly to other areas of conflict around the globe, such as the Middle East. To address this shortcoming, U.S. military leaders created a new joint-service military organization in 1980 called the rapid-deployment joint task force (RDJTF, later to become the Central Command).

Several key requirements were set for the newly formed RDJTF. Ground force elements needed vehicles light enough to be carried on transport aircraft or as a helicopter sling loads. Since the marine and army did not have any armored fighting vehicles that were light or compact enough to fit within the RDJTF guidelines, they searched for an off-the-shelf foreign made light armored vehicle. They wanted a vehicle that was configured to serve many different battlefield roles, and they called it the light armored vehicle (LAV).

A major design benchmark set by the RDJTF for the LAV program called for no vehicle to weigh over 16 tons, the sling-load carrying capacity of the largest U.S. military helicopter at the time. Lightweight armored fighting vehicles have the advantages of such as being more deployable, which was the main goal of the LAV program to begin with. But light weight also carries some disadvantages. Because conventional steel armor is heavy and weight was such a crucial factor in the design of the LAV, its armored protection is proof only up to 7.62mm ball ammunition and 152mm artillery air burst at 17 yards.

After studying many different vehicles, the Marine Corps awarded an initial production contract to General Motors of Canada in September 1982. The LAV that GM Canada submitted to the corps for approval was a license-built copy of an eight-wheeled armored fighting vehicle designed and developed by the Swiss firm of Motorwagenfabrik AG (MOWAG) and called the Piranha I.

Right: **The LAV-25 as pictured is 8 feet 2 1/2-inches tall and 7 feet 2 1/2-inches wide. Besides the M242 25mm automatic cannon mounted in the vehicle's turret, the vehicle comes armed with a coaxial M240 7.62mm machine gun, the barrel of which protrudes from the left side of the 25mm gun tube. On top of the vehicle's turret is another M240 7.62mm machine gun on a pintle mount. On either side of the front of the vehicle's turret are M257 smoke grenade launchers.** Michael Green

Development of the original diesel-powered Piranha I series dated from the 1970s, with the first prototype vehicles appearing in 1972. The marines would eventually obtain funding from Congress to acquire over 800 Canadian-built copies of the Swiss Piranha I and designated them the LAV family of vehicles. There are some minor differences between the marines' LAVs and the original Swiss-designed Piranha I.

In Marine Corps service, the LAV comes in nine different configurations. Four of them are weapon platforms (nicknamed shooters), while the other five are configured to provide support functions. The support function variants of the LAV include the LAV-L (logistics vehicle), the LAV-R (recovery vehicle), the LAV-C2 (command vehicle), the LAV-MEWSS (mobile electronic-warfare support system), and the newest, the LAV-JLNBCRS (joint light nuclear-biological-chemical reconnaissance vehicle). All LAV support vehicles are armed with a pintle-mounted 7.62mm M240 machine gun.

The weapon-carrying versions of the Marine Corps LAV program include the LAV-25 (25mm gun-armed turret), the LAV-AT (antitank), the LAV-AD (air-defense), and the LAV-M (mortar) The corps extensively tested a fifth weapon-armed version of the LAV equipped with a 105mm main gun. However, Congress never provided funding for its procurement.

The Marine Corps committed funding to upgrade its entire family of LAV vehicles with a service life extension program (SLEP) in 2002. It will extend the useful life of the LAV family of vehicles until 2015. In addition to adding several important survivability enhancements and electrical system upgrades the SLEP will replace the passive night sight on the LAV-25 with a more capable thermal imaging sight.

LAV-25

Moving at high speed is a Marine Corps LAV-25. The top speed of the vehicle on a paved level road is 62 miles per hour, but speed can drop to under 15 miles per hour on uneven ground. All eight wheels on the LAV-25 are powered and independently sprung, with coil springs on the front four and torsion bars on the rear four. Power steering applies only to the front four wheels. GM Defense

The LAV-25 has a three-man crew: a vehicle commander and gunner who sit side by side in the vehicle's power-operated turret, and a driver who sits in the left front hull. Mounted in the vehicle's turret is an M242 25mm automatic cannon, called the Chain Gun, and two 7.62mm M240 machine guns, one of which is mounted coaxially along-side the Chain Gun, the other in mounted on a pintle mount in front of the vehicle commander's overhead hatch. The vehicle also comes equipped with a seven-power thermal day/night sight that provides the vehicle commander and gunner with the ability to see potential enemy targets at a range of 4,400 yards. The Marine Corps acquired 422 examples of the LAV-25 between 1983 and 1987.

The 25mm Chain Gun on the LAV-25 is a high-velocity, flat-trajectory, rifled automatic gun. It can engage and destroy lightly armored vehicles, troops in the open, anti-

tank emplacements, and even low-flying planes and heli-copters. It is an externally powered, electric-motor-driven weapon with a maximum effective range against point targets of over 3,000 yards. A dual ammunition feeder permits the gunner to choose between armored-piercing discarding sabot-tracer (APDS-T) ammunition for hard targets or a high-explosive incendiary tracer (HEI-T) for soft targets. The electric motor that drives the gun's ammunition feeder and bolt allows the weapon to fire either single shots or 100 to 200 rounds per minute.

The Marine Corps CH-53E Super Stallion transport heli-copter pictured has as a sling-load a 14-ton LAV-25. The ability to move the LAV-25 and other members of the LAV family of vehicles by helicopter proved to be a crucial requirement for the original design of the vehicle. Besides carrying oversize cargo such as the LAV-25, the Super Stallion is large enough to transport more than 56 fully equipped marines at a normal cruising speed of 173 miles per hour. GM Defense

Pictured is a Marine Corps LAV-25 in the water traveling at its maximum water speed of 6 1/2-miles per hour. Unlike the much larger tracked amphibious assault vehicles (AAVs) that can operate in open ocean water and 10-foot surf, the LAV-25 can operate in swimming mode only in calm inland waterways. To prevent water from spilling over the front hull a large trim vane is stored under the front of the vehicle's hull that is manually erected by the crew prior to insertion into the water. Defense Visual Information Center

The LAV-25 pictured belongs to the Thirteenth MEU and is 21 feet long. Two of the vehicle's four scouts have opened their overhead hatches in the rear hull compartment to give the vehicle all-around observation capabilities. The vehicle pictured has had its propellers and rudders removed to avoid damage during training exercises. Visible on the upper-left-side hull is an emergency hatch. Also, visible are the LAV-25's two large rear doors. Michael Green

Below: Pictured is the light armored vehicle-antitank (LAV-AT) with it's TOW 2 armed turret in the stored position on the vehicle's rear deck. Also visible in this picture are the positions for three of the vehicle's four-man crew. The driver is in the very front of the hull, the vehicle commander's elevated position is behind the driver, and the gunner's turret with an overhead hatch is behind the vehicle commander. GM Defense

The rear hull compartment of the LAV-25 has room for up to six infantrymen. The Marine Corps does not, however, use the LAV-25 as an infantry-fighting vehicle (IFV), like the army's M2 Bradley, since it lacks an adequate amount of armor protection and troop density to perform the types of missions normally assigned to a mechanized infantry unit. Rather, the marines use the LAV-25 as a reconnaissance asset in their light armored reconnaissance (LAR) battalions. Each LAR battalion in the corps has 60 of the LAV-25s. Each of the four companies that comprise the LAR battalion has 14 LAV-25s.

As a reconnaissance vehicle, the LAV-25 normally carries only four marine infantrymen, called scouts, in the rear hull compartment. The corps considers the four scouts assigned to each LAV-25 an integral part of the vehicle's employment, with the vehicle crew and the scouts depending on each other for security, mobility, and firepower. The scouts, who are armed with M4 carbines or the M249 SAWs, perform a wide variety of jobs, such as manning observation posts (OPs), conducting dismounted reconnaissance of close terrain that cannot be bypassed, providing dismounted security at danger areas, and marking contaminated areas and bypasses.

LAV-AT

Shown in this picture of a Marine Corps LAV-AT is the upper part of the TOW under-armor (TUA) turret tilting down the rear of the vehicle's hull to be reloaded. The loader in the rear hull compartment opens the overhead hatch as seen in this picture and inserts fresh missiles into the two TOW 2 missile launchers. The loader then closes his overhead hatch, and the gunner raises the TUA to its fully upright position and points the front of it at the enemy.
Defense Visual Information Center

Because the LAV-25 has no way of defending itself from heavily armored tanks, every LAR battalion has 16 examples of the LAV-AT. The LAV-AT has a power operated turret that contains two TOW 2 missile launchers and the gunner's sighting equipment. The sighting equipment consists of a 12-power thermal sight that can engage enemy tanks during periods of reduced visibility to the range of the missile. The builders of the power-operated turret mounted on the LAV-AT refer to it as the TOW under-armor (TUA) turret.

The upper part of the TUA, or armored launcher assembly, rotates 360-degrees and raises or lowers through a hydraulic trunnion assembly. It was nicknamed the Hammerhead. When the LAV-AT is moving, the Hammerhead is stored on the rear deck of the vehicle's hull in a rear-ward facing position. When the vehicle's gunner, located in the hull of the vehicle, prepares to fire the TOW missiles, the Hammerhead rises with the front of the TOW missiles pointed at the target. In its raised position the Hammerhead extends 5 feet above the vehicle's hull. This gives the LAV-AT crew the ability to keep the

vehicle's hull under cover when engaging targets and gives them a platform capable of firing future generation antitank missiles. The marines hope to field a new and improved version of the LAV-AT by 2009.

When the gunner on the LAV-AT has fired the two ready-round missiles in the Hammerhead, it tilts rearward and is reloaded through an overhead hatch on the roof of the vehicles rear hull compartment. The LAV-AT can carry 14 extra TOW 2 missiles in the rear hull compartment. If the vehicle becomes disabled, a TOW 2 ground-mount kit and a laser range finder are stowed in the vehicle. Besides the gunner, the LAV-AT is crewed by a driver, vehicle commander, and a loader. Normally, a 7.62mm M240 machine gun is mounted on the vehicle commander's cupola in front of the Hammerhead. The Marine Corps acquired 96 LAV-ATs.

Of the LAV family of vehicles, the LAV-AT has proven to be the biggest disappointment to the corps. Excessive corrosion problems from design defects, which have resulted in decreasing readiness rates. In addition, one of the most serious problems has been the excessive

A Marine Corps LAV-AT is pictured parked on a road during a lull in a training exercise. All four members of the vehicle's crew are visible, including the loader standing on the top of the rear hull. Normally, the loader is confined to the rear hull compartment of the vehicle. The upper part of the TOW under-armor (TUA) turret rotates around the gunner's fixed turret. In this picture, the front of the launcher is pointed rearward.
Defense Visual Information Center

With very limited armor protection, the best place for a marine **LAV-AT** to be when engaging enemy tanks is under cover. The crew of the LAV-AT pictured has done just that and has taken a hull-down firing position in a wooded area, using the shadows of surrounding trees to break up the outline of their vehicle. To add to the effect, the crew has also added some branches to the exterior of their vehicle. Defense Visual Information Center

Manning a roadblock during Operation Iraqi Freedom in 2003, a marine **LAV-AT** has its TOW under-armor (TUA) turret in its raised firing position. Clearly seen are the two circular openings for the TOW 2 missile launch tubes. Between the missile launch tubes are the various optical sights and the missile in-flight tracker device that allows the vehicle's gunner to identify targets and then direct wire-guided TOW 2 missiles to them. U.S. Marine Corps

flight time of the wire-guided TOW 2 missiles when engaging targets at their maximum range. Since the gunner on the LAV-AT can only fire and control one TOW 2 missile at a time, the vehicle and crew can remain exposed for up to 2 minutes while firing. In comparison, a well-trained M1A1 Abrams tank crew can load and fire up to 12 120mm main gun rounds within 60 seconds at a variety of different targets.

Pictured on alert for hostile aircraft is a four-vehicle platoon of light armored vehicle-air defense (LAV-AD) variants. Like all members of the LAV family of vehicles the LAV-AD is powered by a six-cylinder General Motors diesel engine coupled to an Allison MT653 transmission with five forward speeds and one reverse. General Dynamics Armament Systems

The LAV-AD air-defense variant of the LAV did not enter Marine Corps service until 1997. While the original requirement called for production of 125 examples of the LAV-AD, in the end, Congress would fund production of only 17 vehicles. This allowed the forming of a single LAV-AD platoon, which comprises four sections, each of which has four LAV-AD vehicles and a single LAV-L. The remaining LAV-AD vehicles serve as replacements.

Because the Corps does not have enough LAV-ADs to equip every Marine Expeditionary Unit (MEU) deployed overseas, the vehicles serve as a Marine Expeditionary Force (MEF) asset. However, if the need arose, elements of the LAV-AD platoon have the ability to be transported by air to help support an MEU that called for their protection.

The LAV-AD has a two-man, power-operated turret, on top of which is the main armament, eight ready-to-fire Stinger surface-to-air missiles housed in two separate missile launching pods. The LAV-AD carries an additional eight Stinger missiles in its rear hull compartment as reloads. In a pinch, the missile can engage ground targets.

As a secondary weapon, the vehicle's turret is armed with a GAU-12/U 25mm Gatling gun. It has 385 ready rounds, with storage space inside the vehicle for another 605 reload rounds. The 25mm Gatling gun's intended role is to engage aerial targets flying within the Stinger's minimum launch distance, or nearby ground targets. While the gun can fire up to 1,800 rounds per minute, it is normally fired in bursts of 10, 30, 60, or 100 rounds, which are set by a burst-selector switch in the vehicle.

The LAV-ADs operate in four-vehicle sections close behind leading LAV-25 units to ensure early engagement of approaching hostile aircraft. Information on enemy aircraft is passed from outside radar units to the LAV-AD section through a data link to the vehicles' radios. The LAV-AD vehicles themselves have a television/forward looking infrared (TV/FLIR) sight in the vehicle's turret to identify enemy aircraft. If this system loses power, the LAV-AD crew has a fixed, manual backup sight to engage targets. They also have an eye-safe laser rangefinder to detect targets out to range of 6.2 miles. This information, aside from input from other sensors, is fed into onboard computer systems that automatically provide the correct lead and elevation for both the vehicles' Stinger missiles, and 25mm Gatling gun.

Just the tip of the muzzle of an 81mm mortar protrudes from the center of the upper hull of a Marine Corps light armored vehicle-mortar (LAV-M) variant. Visible on the upper part of the front hull is a 15,000-pound, self-recovery winch normally found on all versions of LAV vehicles. Just under the winch on the lower front part of the hull is the vehicle's aluminum trim vane in its stored position, which is also common to all versions of the LAV. GM Defense

LAV-M

A picture of an LAV-M variant shows the closed three-section hatch on the roof of the vehicle's hull. The hatch protects the three-man mortar crew from overhead artillery, mortar burst, fragments, and the elements. The thin vertical piece of metal installed in front of the driver's position snags any wires or cables strung across the vehicle's path so crewmembers who may stick their heads out of their hatches won't be decapitated. GM Defense

The Marine Corps currently has an inventory of 50 LAV-Ms in service. They are armed with an M252 81mm mortar mounted in the center of the vehicle's hull on a 360-degree rotating turntable. A three-section hatch in the hull roof of the LAV-M opens to allow the vehicle's crew to raise the 81mm mortar into its vertical firing position, making the mortar protrude slightly above the top of the hull. In transit, the three-section hatch closes, and the 81mm mortar is lowered onto its rotating turntable.

The LAV-M, has space for 90 rounds of 81mm ammunition. The normal mix of mortar ammunition consists of 68 high-explosive (HE) rounds, nine smoke rounds, and 13 illuminating rounds. The crew of five includes a driver, a vehicle commander, and a three-man mortar squad. The mortar squad has fold-down seats on the right side of the rear hull compartment. The entrance or egress for the mortar crew is through two large doors at the rear of the vehicle's hull. Besides the 81mm mortar, the LAV-M is also armed with an M240 7.62mm machine gun on the commander's cupola to protect the vehicle.

Pictured in a training exercise in the desolate desert waste of Marine Corps Air-Ground Combat Center at Twentynine Palms, California, is an LAV-M variant. Like all versions of LAVs, the LAV-M can travel up a 60 percent grade or operate along a 30-degree side slope. It can also cross a trench 5.7 feet long or drive over a vertical wall almost 20 inches tall. Greg Stewart

To increase indirect firepower available to a LAR battalion, the Marine Corps is exploring the choice of mounting a more powerful and longer-ranged 120mm mortar on an LAV chassis. The corps is calling the 120mm mortar in development Dragon Fire. Dragon Fire will be an effective force multiplier because of its ability to utilize precision targeting systems that will soon enter the corps inventory. Experiments with a French-designed, 120mm mortar mounted on an LAV chassis have already shown positive results.

Weapon-armed Humvees

In the early 1980s, the corps began pulling out of service its fleet of M151-series 1/4-ton tactical trucks and M274 series 1/2-ton trucks known as mechanical mules (both of which served as platforms to mount a variety of weapons) The mules were replaced by high mobility multipurpose wheeled vehicles (HMMWVs). Since HMMWV is a mouthful to pronounce, the vehicle is nicknamed the Humvee or Hummer. (Humvee is a registered trademark of AM General. Hummer is a registered trademark of General Motors and applies only to civilian versions of the vehicle.)

The greatest number of Humvees in Corps service today are the non-armored, cargo-troop carriers. They have plastic-covered enclosures and plastic-covered, metal-frame doors with clear plastic windows. The front windshields are made from polycarbonate bullet-resistant glass, and, depending on the mission and weather, cargo-troop-carrier Humvees are either open- or close-topped. While not normally thought of as weapon carriers, the Humvee cargo-troop carriers can mount a weapon-station for various types of machine guns.

Four slightly different versions of the Humvee are configured as weapon carriers and are in corps service in smaller numbers. These versions have a permanent, hard-top, steel-armor enclosure that covers them from the front windshield to the rear tailgate. They include the M1043A2 armament carrier and an identical version with a winch

A group of marines from the Twentyfourth MEU are pictured driving through a checkpoint during Operation Iraqi Freedom. They are riding on a non-armored version of the Humvee designated the M1038A1 cargo-troop carrier. Since they might be subjected to enemy fire at any moment, the marines on board have their personnel weapons at the ready. Staff Sergeant Bryan P. Reed

Looking for a fight is this heavily armed Marine Corps armament carrier variant armed with a TOW 2 antitank missile launcher and a M240G 7.62mm machine gun on the roof of the vehicle. It's pictured passing through the Iraqi city of An-Nasiriyah during Operation Iraqi Freedom in 2003. The crew stands ready to return fire from any direction. Lance Corporal Gordon A. Rouse

The M1043A1 armament carrier version of the marine Corps Humvee pictured is armed with a pintle-mounted M2 .50-caliber machine gun. Several exterior features of the Marine Corps Humvees distinguish it from those used by the other services. They include a deep water fording kit consisting of an exhaust-pipe extension that runs all to the vehicle's top rear driver's side. On the passenger's side is an extended air intake pipe behind the hood. Michael Green

Taking part in a training exercise is a marine armament carrier armed with a TOW 2 antitank missile launcher. The armament carrier versions of the Humvee are about 6 feet high, 15 feet long, and 7 feet wide. Like all military Humvees, they have an independent suspension system, front and rear, with double A-arms, coil springs, and double acting shock absorbers front and back. Michael Green

designated the M1044A2 armament carrier. These vehicles can mount a variety of weapons such as the M2HB .50-caliber machine gun, the Mk. 19 grenade launcher, or the M240 7.62mm machine gun. The guns are mounted on a 32 inch weapon ring with a pintle mount and a quick-release cradle located on the vehicle's roof.

The other weapon carriers in marine service are the M1045A2 TOW carrier and the identical M1046A2 TOW carrier with winch. They are designed to carry the four-man TOW missile crew with the complete weapon and its associated equipment. The storage space in the rear of the vehicles has room for six TOW 2 reload missiles.

Pictured on patrol in southern Afghanistan is a marine Corps Humvee armament carrier. It is armed with a TOW 2 antitank missile launcher with an M240G 7.62mm machine gun on the roof. Marine Corps armament carriers have thin, flat, steel armor plates attached to their doors, which are not seen on armament carriers of the other services. This feature and the deep water fording kit are the easiest way to spot a marine Corps armament carrier. Sergeant Joseph R. Chenelly

A large folding tripod carried in the vehicles is used when the TOW 2 launcher needs to be fired from the ground.

In civilian terms, the Humvee weapon carriers in corps service are hatchback models. Their doors are made from aluminum and fiberglass with polycarbonate bullet-resistant windows that roll up and down. A composite fiber liner known as E-glass is embedded in the doors of the weapon carriers to resist small-caliber bullet fragments. The front windshields consist of polycarbonate bullet-resistant glass, and the hood vents have baffles to prevent bullet fragments from damaging the engine. Because the marines wanted more protection for the crews of its weapon carriers, AM General equipped them with an added supplemental armor kit consisting of thin, flat steel armor plates attached to the doors and other surfaces.

THE AVENGER

Reflecting the versatility of the Humvee chassis as a weapon carrier, a specialized antiaircraft-missile-armed version of the vehicle, in corps service known as the Avenger, consists of an electrically driven, one-man, rotating armored turret mounted on the rear platform of the M1037 shelter carrier version of the Humvee. On either side of the turret are armored launcher pods, each containing four ready-to-fire Stinger antiaircraft missiles.

When the Avenger activates, it takes less than 15 seconds to ready the missiles for firing. Aiming the Avenger comes from either the gunner's direct vision or from a forward looking infrared (FLIR) system. The two-man Avenger crew can fire its missiles on the move or operate the missile system from a distance of 55 yards with the aid of a remote-control device. Besides the eight ready-to-fire Stingers in the launcher pods, the vehicle has storage space for eight reload missiles. Once the Avenger crew fires its initial load of eight missiles, it takes less than four minutes to complete the reloading process.

For engaging aerial targets within the minimum firing range of the Stingers, a Belgian-designed M3P .50-caliber machine gun is mounted under one of the two missile launcher pods. The air-cooled, recoil-operated machine

The Stinger missile pods mounted on either side of the turret of the Avenger air defense system can elevate up to 70 degrees and depress 10 degrees. Seen in the open position on this Avenger is the gunner's large transparent canopy, which allows the gunner to both see his targets as well as aim the onboard missiles. Under the right-hand Stinger missile pod are the gunner's day and night optical sighting systems and eye-safe laser range finder. Lance Corporal Nathaniel C. Le Blanc

Pictured in traveling order is a marine avenger air defense system. To protect the gunner's large transparent canopy and two Stinger missile pods from the effects of the sun and dust from off-road use, the crew covers them with protective wraps. To protect the Avenger's day and night optical sighting system, found under the right-side missile pod, a metal enclosure fits over them as seen in this picture. Michael Green

Installed under one of the two Stinger missile pods found on the Avenger air defense system is an M3P .50-caliber air-cooled machine gun. It is a Belgian-designed-and-built upgrade of the reliable M2 .50-caliber machine gun. It weighs about 80 pounds and is 65 inches long with a rate of fire of 950 to 1,100 rounds per minute, nearly double that of the older M2 .50-caliber machine gun. Mounted on the Avenger the M3P has 200 ready rounds of ammunition. Lance Corporal Nathaniel C. LeBlanc

gun is fed from a magazine containing 200 rounds. Besides aerial targets, the M3P .50-caliber machine gun can be used against a variety of ground targets. The Avenger went into full-scale production in April 1988 and is built by Boeing Aerospace Company. The main mission of the Avenger is to counter hostile, low-flying, high-speed, fixed-wing aircraft and helicopters attacking Marine Corps units.

FAST-ATTACK VEHICLES

In the late 1980s, the army began testing many different vehicles to determine their fitness for use with a new type of light infantry division. One of the vehicles tested was a militarized dune buggy designed and built by the Chenowth Racing Company and designated as a fast

attack vehicle (FAV). While the army eventually decided that FAVs were not suitable for its light infantry divisions, the Navy SEALs and the Marine Corps decided that the vehicle could serve some useful purposes. The marines thought FAVs would work well with its raiding forces and ground reconnaissance teams.

Since there were few FAVs to begin with, the marines had to improvise. In 1988, they developed their own version of the vehicle based on the chassis of an outdated M151A2 1/4-ton tactical truck. Converting 121 M151A2s into FAVs called for the replacement of their original narrow tires with commercially available wider tires and wheels. The new wider tires protruded beyond the width

Pictured taking part in a parade in the United States following the first Gulf War, is a marine fast attack vehicle (FAV) armed with an M2 .50-caliber machine gun. The M151 series 1/4-ton tactical truck, which the FAV is based on, first entered production in 1960 and was built for the U.S. armed forces until 1988. During its long career with the marines, the FAV saw use in many different configurations, including armed variants. The FAV was merely the last in service with the marines. Defense Visual Information Center

With a growing need to seek out a suitable replacement for its tired inventory of M151-based fast attack vehicles (FAVs), the Marine Corps turned to General Dynamics Land System Division (GDLS). The firm soon began work on the developing a next-generation wheeled vehicle narrow enough to fit in the interior confines of the corps' existing fleet of transport helicopters. The result is the strange-looking vehicle pictured called the Shadow, or the reconnaissance surveillance targeting vehicle (RST-V). General Dynamics Land Systems Division

of the vehicle's original fenders, so rubber mud guards were added. Other additions included wire stowage racks, rear side shields, thick roll bars, and a variety of weapons, including M2 .50-caliber machine guns and even TOW II missile launchers.

Despite their age and maintenance problems and the fact that they used very flammable unleaded fuel, the M151A2 FAVs were popular with the marines because they were small and narrow enough to fit in a CH-46 transport helicopter. Two could fit in the larger CH-53 transport helicopter. This gave the marines instant tactical mobility immediately after the helicopters carrying them touched down and dropped their large rear ramp. By 1997, the M151A2 FAVs were wearing out from hard use and needed to be replaced.

To replace the M151A2 FAV and the various weapon-armed versions of the Humvee in reconnaissance, the Marine Corps in 1997 began to develop a deep-reconnaissance vehicle designated the reconnaissance, surveillance, targeting vehicle (RST-V), also known as the Shadow. General Dynamics Land Systems (GDLS) has undertaken development of the vehicle for the Marine Corps.

In early prototypes, the Shadow was a low-slung, four-wheel, hybrid-electric-drive vehicle with integrated stealth and survivability features. Under current plans, the vehicle's chassis will serve many different roles, including weapon carrier, light-strike vehicle, command-post vehicle, NBC Reconnaissance vehicle, forward-air-control vehicle, and ambulance. Instead of restricting the width of the Shadow to fit in current marine corps transport helicopters or the upcoming V-22 Osprey tilt-rotor aircraft, the width of the vehicle is adjustable with a unique foldout suspension system that allows the Shadow to be as narrow as an M151 FAV or as wide as a Humvee for better off-road stability.

THE SHADOW

As a hybrid electric drive vehicle, the Shadow has significantly improved fuel economy over existed wheeled vehicles in the corps inventory. Besides having the ability to adjust its width, the vehicle's height can also be lowered using its pneumatic suspension system. These features allow the Shadow to be driven on and off the corps' CH-53 and CH-46 transport helicopters, V-22 Osprey tilt-rotor aircraft, and C-130 Hercules transport planes. Twenty-one Shadows will fit in the air force's massive C-5A Galaxy transport plane and 12 fit in the new C-17 Globemaster II transport plane. General Dynamics Land Systems Division

The newest wheeled fighting vehicle in the marine arsenal is the interim fast attack vehicle (IFAV). The example pictured has as its main armament an M240G 7.62mm machine gun mounted to fire over the removable cab. The vehicle also carries several Javelin antitank missiles in its rear cargo bay. Like all the corps' wheeled vehicles, the IFAV has a deep water fording kit. The extended air-intake pipe is mounted on the front hood of the vehicle shown. Michael Green

Because it could be several years before the Marine Corps fields the Shadow, in 1999 the corps fielded an interim fast attack vehicle (IFAV). The vehicle chosen for the role was a DaimlerChrysler model of the Mercedes-Benz MB 290 GD 1 1/2-ton off-road truck. The four-wheel-drive, diesel-powered pickup truck was first used in German army service. Like the M151A2 FAV, the IFAV is small and narrow enough to be carried in the corps' larger transport helicopters as well as the planned V-22 Osprey. Ninety-two examples of the IFAV are now in corps service.

The IFAV has many features that quickly made the marines assigned to the vehicles its biggest fans. Besides an air-conditioned, two-person cab, it has an automatic five-speed transmission. The vehicle's top speed is 97 miles per hour, with a range of 540 miles. The IFAV's outstanding off-road mobility allows it to climb an 80 percent grade. Besides the two-man cab, the IFAV can carry up to four marines with all their weapons and equipment in its rear cargo bay. The only armor on the vehicle is a shrapnel-proof floor that will resist certain types of hand grenades. The IFAV can mount, on a specially designed lightweight pedestal, everything from the 7.62mm M240 machine gun to the Mk. 19 automatic grenade launcher. A TOW 2 launcher can also be mounted on the vehicle.

Driven out of the rear cargo door of a Marine Corps CH-53 Super Stallion transport helicopter is an IFAV. To fit in the tight confines of the helicopter's cargo compartment, the IFAV has a width of just over 5 feet and a height with its roll bar folded down of a little over 5 feet. The vehicle is powered by a 270-ci, Mercedes-Benz inline five-cylinder, turbocharged, diesel engine that produces 156 horsepower. U.S. Marine Corps

In Southern Iraq, a Marine Corps IFAV from the Force Reconnaissance Detachment of the Fifteenth MEU (SOC), stands guard by the United Nations (UN) complex near Umm Qasr during Operation Iraqi Freedom. The marine in the vehicle's rear cargo bay is aiming an M2 .50-caliber machine gun at a possible target. Notice the attached laser-aiming device mounted on a bracket on top of the weapon's receiver. Strapped to the side of the vehicle is an AT-4 antitank weapon. The marine aiming over the hood of the IFAV is armed with an M249 5.56mm SAW. Lance Corporal Brian L. Wickliffe

TRACKED WEAPON-EQUIPPED VEHICLES

Pictured on display at the Military Vehicle Technology Foundation (MVTF) museum is an example of a 6-ton tank M1917 as used by the corps in the 1920s. The hull and turret of the vehicle were a bolted assembly of flat, face-hardened, steel armor plates held with commercial angle iron. The driver could enter the vehicle through three doors in the front hull. The vehicle commander/gunner entered the vehicle through small doors in the rear of the turret. Michael Green

The first tank in Marine Corps service was the World War I-era 6 ton M1917. With a crew of two, it had a top speed of about 5 1/2 miles per hour and was armed with either a 37mm main gun or a Browning .30-caliber air-cooled machine gun. The marines borrowed three of them from the army in 1923, and by the end of the 1920s the corps had eight of the M1917s in service. A lack of interest and money caused the corps to disband its tank force in November of 1928.

Above: **The last version of the M4 series of medium tanks in corps service was designated the medium tank M4A3 (105) HVSS. The vehicle pictured is an M4A3 (105) in corps markings. It is owned by vehicle collector and former marine tanker Fred Ropkey, who commanded a platoon of five M4s during his time in service and always remembered the tanks fondly. Hence, his interest in restoring a surplus example to its original condition minus the working armament.** Michael Green

In 1934, the marines once again considered adding tanks to their inventory. Experiments conducted in the following years involved up to 10 machine-gun-armed, turret-less light tanks designed and built by the Marmon-Herrington Company. The light tanks showed promise. However, the firm did not have the production facilities needed to fulfill a 1940 the Marine Corps order for 36 CTL-3 light tanks. The corps was forced to borrow 36 examples of the M2A4 light tank from the army. A number of Marmon-Herrington light tanks, totaling no more than 30, were in corps service early in World War II, but all were discarded by 1943.

The four-man M2A4 light tank weighed roughly 11 tons and was armed with a turret-mounted 37mm main gun and up to five M1919A4 .30-caliber machine guns. The American Car and Foundry Company and Baldwin Locomotive Works built the M2A4 light tank. The vehicle would see marine combat action in 1942 before being replaced by an improved version of the vehicle designated the M3 light tank. The M3 series would remain the standard marine light tank until late 1943 when the M5A1 replaced it. Both M3 series and M5A1 light tanks had four-man crews and were armed with a turret-mounted 37mm main gun. The M3 and M5 series of light tanks were typically armed with three M1919A4 .30-caliber machine guns.

Because the 37mm main gun on the various light tanks used by the Marine Corps in the Pacific did not pack enough punch to deal with well-built Japanese defensive positions, the marines soon opted for the M4 medium tank series in late 1942. The M4 offered a more powerful turret-mounted 75mm main gun that fired not only a very effective armor-piercing main gun round, but also a very potent high-explosive main gun round. The M4 series of medium tanks is probably best known by its British military nickname, the Sherman. American tankers simply referred to the vehicle as the M4.

In addition to the 75mm main gun, the five-man, 32-ton M4 series of medium tanks carried up to three machine guns. One M1919A4 .30-caliber machine gun was co-axially mounted in the turret and the other was fitted in a ball mount on the front of the hull. An M2 .50-caliber machine gun could also be mounted on the roof of the vehicle. Another version of the M4 medium-tank series used by the corps came configured as a flame-thrower vehicle.

After World War II, the only version of the M4 retained by the corps mounted an 105mm howitzer and was designated the M4A3 (105) HVSS. The letters *HVSS* stood for horizontal volute spring suspension system. This variant of the M4 series saw service with the corps during the Korean War and was finally retired in 1959.

Postwar Tanks

The marines put the 42 ton M26 Pershing medium tank into service in 1948. The five-man tank was armed with a turret-mounted 90mm main gun and would see combat action during the Korean War until 1951, when it was replaced by an upgraded model designated the M46 Patton tank. The M46 weighed about 46 tons and was armed with an improved version of the 90mm main gun. Like the M26, the M46 would see marine combat during the Korean War, after which the M47 Patton medium tank replaced it. Like its predecessors, the M47 had a five-man crew and was armed with a 90mm main gun.

Because it was rushed into service, the M47 suffered from many design problems. Despite these problems, the tank would remain in service until 1959. Its replacement was the 50-ton M48A1 medium tank, which began appearing in field service in 1955. The M48A1 was a refined version of the M47 with a new turret design carrying the same 90mm main gun. Unlike the M47, the M48A1 had only a four-man crew. Like the M26 Pershing and the earlier versions of the Patton tank series, the M48A1 was powered by a gasoline engine.

In late 1964, a diesel-powered version of the M48 Patton tank series entered service. It was designated the M48A3 Patton medium tank. The marines now had a vehicle that was less prone to the disastrous fires that plagued gasoline-powered equipment caused by the high flammability of gasoline. The M48A3 had a four-man crew and was the mainstay of the corps tank fleet for many years. It saw heavy combat action during the Vietnam War, where the vehicle earned a reputation as a dependable and reliable fighting machine.

The marines also used flamethrowing versions of their M48A1 and M48A3 medium tanks. This variant was designated the M67 and M67A2 full-tracked combat tank, flamethrower. The M67A2 version saw action with the marines during the Vietnam War and remained in service until 1972.

Pictured on a naval landing craft are three Marine Corps M48A3 Patton medium tanks of B Company, Third Marine Tank Battalion. The date is March 9, 1965, and the location is just off the coast of Da Nang, South Vietnam. All three tanks have deep water fording kits. Notice the extended engine exhaust pipes sticking up from the vehicle's rear hull. M48A3 Patton tanks would serve in support of marine infantry units during the Vietnam War until late 1969. U.S. Marine Corps

Marines from the First Tank Battalion wait aboard their M60A1 RISE/Passive tanks for firing to resume while taking part in live-fire training during Operation Desert Shield. Desert Shield was the buildup of U.S. forces in the Middle East prior to the United States' first war with Iraq in 1991 that became known as Operation Desert Storm. The last M60A1 RISE/Passive tank ended service in 1994. Defense Visual Information Center

Taking part in a training exercise is a Marine Corps M60A1 RISE/Passive tank from C Company of the First Tank Battalion. It is pictured fitted with dummy reactive armor tiles on both its hull and turret to simulate the size and weight of the real thing. The authentic reactive armor tiles, each of which contained a small explosive charge used for deflecting incoming shape-charge warheads, remained in storage for safety reasons and was mounted on the tanks only when committed to combat. Greg Stewart

The M48A3 remained in corps service until it was replaced by early production models of the M60A1 main battle tank in 1975. Powered by a diesel engine, the 50-ton vehicle was armed with a British-designed 105mm main gun. Unlike the hemispherical turrets on the M48 series medium tanks, and the original version of the M60 tank, the M60A1 turret featured an elongated nose that provided better ballistic protection from enemy armor-piercing rounds.

In 1977 the corps replaced its early model M60A1s with an upgraded version known as the M60A1 RISE/Passive. The term RISE stands for reliability-improved-selected-equipment engine. The term *passive* refers to the improved passive periscope sights for the tank commander and gunner.

To improve the protection level of its M60A1 RISE/Passive tanks from shape-charge warheads, the corps added explosive reactive armor tiles beginning in 1988. The M60A1 would see combat service with the corps in the 1983 U.S. invasion of Grenada and the U.S. involvement in Lebanon between 1982 and 1984. The vehicle also saw action in the first Gulf War, Operation Desert Storm, in 1991.

THE M103 HEAVY TANK

In 1945, the Soviet Union fielded a new heavy tank that presented an immediate challenge to all NATO forces, including U.S. forces deployed in Western Europe. Weighing 46 tons, the IS-3 (also known as the Stalin tank) benefited from an innovative hull design and a 122mm main gun. The 60-ton U.S. M103 heavy tank was designed to meet the challenge. It was also heavily armored and mounted a 120mm main gun. Of the 300 M103s produced, 220 were eventually allocated to the marines in 1964.

While hardly an ideal vehicle for amphibious operations, the M103's heavy armor and large-caliber main gun were important attributes to an organization dependent on effective infantry support. In time, the Marine Corps would fund an upgraded M103A1 version, and later the M103A2. The most successful variant was the M103A2, which mounted the same gun and armor as its predecessors, but benefited from some improvements, including a simpler diesel engine and enlarged fuel tanks that dramatically increased the tank's cruising range to almost 300 miles.

Very slowly and carefully a 60-ton M103A1 heavy tank armed with a 120mm main gun is pictured driving off a navy landing craft in 1962. Due to the size and weight of the 120mm ammunition, it did not fire a fixed round. Instead, it used separate loading ammunition with the projectile and propellant cartridge loaded sequentially into the gun's breech prior to firing. To help speed up the loading process, the M103 was the only U.S. tank ever built that had two loaders. Gene Berbaum

The M103A2 passed from corps service in 1973 due to the planned introduction of the M60A1 tank in 1974. The 105mm main gun on the M60A1 had a performance level similar to the 120mm main gun on the M103A2, and the armor-protection level on the two tanks was also very similar. The fact that the M60A1 could do everything the M103A2 could do, was lighter by 10 tons, and had better mobility, made the heavier tank obsolete. With the retirement of the last U.S. heavy tank, the terms *medium* and *heavy* no longer applied in tank nomenclature. At this point, the term "main battle tank" came into existence. The eventual replacement for the M60A1 RISE/Passive tanks in corps inventory was the M1A1 Abrams. It was a

THE M1A1 ABRAMS

68-ton vehicle manned by a crew of four and was armed with a powerful main gun and several machine guns. The main engine was a powerful 1,500-horsepower gas turbine. Special composite armor gave the vehicle an unsurpassed level of protection from both shape-charge warheads and armor-piercing rounds.

The M1A1 was the third version of the Abrams tank series to enter U.S. military service. The first version of the Abrams was the M1, which began army field use in 1982. It was armed with the same 105mm main gun mounted on the M60A1 tank. The M1 was followed into army service two years later by the improved-performance M1 (IPM1), which featured improvements to its armor, final drive, suspension system, and outside stowage racks. The IPM1 was still armed with a 105mm main gun. It took until 1986 before the M1A1 entered army field service. The key change to the vehicle was the replacement of the 105mm rifled main gun with a U.S.-built version of a German-designed 120mm smooth bore main gun that offered superior range and penetration.

Along with the new 120mm main gun and the upgraded fire-control computer system, the M1A1 received better armor protection and a nuclear, biological, chemical (NBC) overpressure system designed to keep contaminated air out of the crew compartment. The new main gun and a series of improvements to the armor increased the weight of the M1A1 and put extra burden on the suspension, transmission and final drives, which also received upgrades effective with the first M1A1 tanks.

Prime contractor General Dynamic Land Systems (GDLS) produced the M1A1 between 1985 and 1993. During that period, the company continued to make minor improvements to the vehicle's design based on research and user feedback. The most dramatic improvement to the M1A1 entered production in 1988 when the composite turret armor was upgraded with a layer of depleted uranium (DU). This extremely dense material, a byproduct of nuclear fission, greatly improved the ability of the turret to defeat the latest generation of armor-piercing rounds.

Driving down a Southern California beach is a Marine Corps M1A1 commons tank armed with a 120mm main gun. Besides the main gun, the vehicle comes armed with two M240 7.62mm machine guns. One of the two M240 machine guns mounts alongside the main gun as a coaxial gun. The other gun mounts on a skate ring on the loader hatch. The M1A1 vehicle commander has an M2 .50-caliber machine gun attached to his cupola. Greg Stewart

A Marine Corps M1A1 common tank drives off a navy landing craft. The vehicle is fitted with a track-width, mine-clearing plow, which is normally stowed in the raised position on the front of the vehicle. When a minefield's location is identified, the mine-clearing plow can be lowered from the safety of the tank. As the M1A1 slowly drives into a minefield, the plow digs into the ground about 4 inches, and picks up mines from below, and guides them out to either side of the vehicle without exploding. Greg Stewart

A Marine Corps M1A1 common tank awaits further orders during a training exercise conducted somewhere in the Middle East prior to Operation Iraqi Freedom. Underneath the small tan-covered box on the top of the vehicle's turret is a Sanders missile countermeasures device (MCD) designated the AN/VLQ-8A. It is an electro-optical jammer that disrupts the enemy's semi-automatic command to line-of-sight (SACLOS) antitank guided missiles, laser range finders, and target designators. Petty Officer 2nd Class Jeffrey Lehrberg

The vehicles equipped with DU armor were designated the M1A1 HA. The *HA* is an abbreviation for heavy armor.

In total, GDLS built 4,550 M1A1s, making it the most common version of the Abrams tank in U.S. military service. Of that number, 269 went to the Marine Corps in 1991; these tanks were designated M1A1 common tanks The 1991 M1A1 had more tie-down points, a position location reporting system (PLRS) interface, and a deep water fording kit (DWFK) that increased the vehicle's fording depth from 3 feet to 6 feet with the tank's turret in the forward position. The DWFK consists of two intake pipes and one exhaust pipe that can be erected in less than 60 minutes.

The marines originally planned to acquire 564 M1A1s in 1986, but funding constraints made that schedule impossible. This was not the first time that inadequate funding hampered the corps' acquisition of Abrams tanks. As early as 1981, the marines had tried to replace their outdated M60A1 RISE/Passive tanks with M1 tanks with-

out success. This continued until 1990, when a revised plan called for the marines to receive the first 16 M1A1 tanks for training. Between 1991 and 1992, the marines completed the transition from M60A1 RISE/Passive tanks to the new M1A1s, with the first Gulf War greatly accelerating the M1A1 transition program.

During the buildup for Operation Desert Shield, the Marine Corps' small tank fleet received a supplement of 60 M1A1 HA tanks from the army's inventory. The marines engaged the Iraqi army with a combination of those 60 borrowed M1A1 HAs and 16 newly built Marine Corps M1A1 HA/common tanks delivered on an accelerated schedule. The marines also used their aging inventory of M60A1 RISE/Passive tanks. The 76 M1A1 HA tanks saw use with the Second Tank Battalion and elements of the Fourth Tank Battalion. The marines returned the 60 borrowed M1A1 HA tanks to the army at the end of Desert Storm.

A Marine Corps M1A1 common tank fires an antitank training round during a training exercise. In obtaining first-round hits with the vehicle's main gun, the Abrams crew is aided with an integral laser range finder, which aims a pulse of intense light at a chosen target. When the light beam reflects off the object, a receiving lens mounted on the tank picks it up. A computer inside the tank measures the return time and translates that information into a range display for the M1A1 gunner. Lance Corporal G. Lane Miley

Visible in this picture is the muzzle blast from a Marine Corps M1A1 common tank as a projectile goes downrange at more than a mile per second. Inside the Abrams, a very sophisticated digital computer linked with the tank's fire control system accommodates changes in ammunition and ballistics data and provides accurate lead corrections for moving targets. The computer also continually monitors the functioning of the tank's fire-control system for any faults. Corporal Allan J. Grdovich

Congress provided funding to GDLS in 1994 and 1995 to transfer 134 M1A1 tanks to the marines from army inventory, with 84 tanks coming from Camp Shelby, Mississippi. These tanks had been built prior to 1991 and lacked the extra features that marked them as M1A1 common tanks. The remaining 48 tanks came from Fort Hood, Texas; and because they were built after 1991, they met the corps criteria for common tanks.

The corps' inventory of tanks before Operation Iraqi Freedom in early 2003 consisted of 317 M1A1 common tanks and 84 older M1A1 tanks, making a total of 401. The corps lost only three M1A1 tanks during the conflict with Iraq. In early 2003, the army transferred an additional 12 M1A1 common tanks to the marines.

An important improvement to marine M1A1 tanks was replacing the existing AN/VVS-2 passive driver's night sight with a new thermal imaging driver's sight that offers almost the same view that the vehicle commander and gunner have with their turret-mounted thermal sight. The corps refers to this new driver's thermal sight as the armored vehicle driver's vision enhancer. The sight proved to be so useful that it has also been mounted in all marine AAVs, LAVs, armored bridge launcher vehicles, and the M88 series armored recovery vehicles.

To keep pace with the recent developments in precision-guided antitank weapons, the corps has embarked on a program to enhance the battlefield survivability of its M1A1 tanks. The program will run through 2012 and is aimed at keeping the M1A1 tank a viable asset through 2020. Survivability improvements will include detection avoidance (signature management) devices aimed at making the vehicle harder to see on the battlefield by enemy radar or thermal-imaging devices. Other survivability features will include a laser warning receiver that will alert the vehicle's crew to the fact that an enemy laser designator is illuminating (painting) their vehicle. Tied into this laser-warning receiver will be a choice of countermeasure devices to dispute the aim of the laser designator. In addition, the 269 M1A1 HA/common tanks in corps inventory will receive upgraded armor.

The firepower enhancement program (FEP) is another key part of the marine M1A1 improvement program. This is a package of upgrades that will increase the tank crew's ability to detect, recognize, and identify targets. It will increase all-weather engagement ranges, crew situational awareness, and target location accuracy. The system includes a second-generation thermal sight, a north-finding/far-target location capability, and an eye-safe laser range finder. This program started in 1999 and will be fully implemented by 2008.

When the corps is ready to retire its aging inventory of M1A1 tanks and LAVs in 2020, it hopes to begin a planned transition to the brand-new expeditionary family of fighting vehicles (MEFFV). As of 2003, it has not been decided if the marines' future armored fighting vehicles will be wheeled, tracked, or a combination of both. The corps envisions a series of manned combat vehicles weighing between 10 and 30 tons, that are assisted by smaller, unmanned robotic vehicles. The weapons under consideration include guns, guided missiles, laser weapons and electromagnetic guns. The corps and the army, which is intent on fielding its own next-generation armored fighting vehicles in the next 20 years, have already made plans to keep each other informed of their progress to avoid any duplication of effort.

Amphibious Tractors from World War II Through the Vietnam War

The weapon-armed vehicle that best symbolizes the modern marine amphibious warfare role is the amphibious assault vehicle (AAV). The current version descends from a long line of amphibious tractors originally developed by civilian inventor Donald Roebling in the early 1930s. These unique vehicles have had many official and unofficial designations over the years. From World War II through the late 1970s the most common designation was landing vehicle tracked (LVT), in keeping with the navy's nomenclature system for landing craft. Most marines continue to refer to them as amtracs (amphibious tractor) regardless of the version in use.

The first version of the LVT to enter corps service during World War II was the 10-ton LVT1. By the end of that war, American companies had built 15,645 LVTs in many different versions. Some served as armored personnel carriers, while others evolved into fire-support vehicles. After the war, the corps scrapped all the early

The Marine Corps' first amphibious tractor was the unarmored landing vehicle tracked-one (LVT1) as pictured. It weighed about 10 tons and was powered by a water-cooled, Hercules six-cylinder gasoline engine that gave it a top road speed of 12 miles hour. In the water, the LVT1 was restricted to a speed of 6 knots. Its rear cargo bay had room for either 24 infantrymen or 2 more tons of cargo. In the field, some vehicles were fitted with appliqué armor. National Archives

A formation of 19-ton Marine Corps LVT3s is pictured in the water during training. Between 1943 and 1945, almost 3,000 LVT3s came off the production line. They first saw combat with the corps during the battle for Okinawa in April 1945 and were powered by two Cadillac-series, eight-cylinder gasoline engines. Top land speed for the LVT3 was 17 miles per hour with a water speed of about 6 knots. After World War II, the vehicles were rebuilt with a higher deck, overhead cargo hatches, and a machine-gun-armed turret. The upgraded vehicles were designated LVTC3. National Archives

The first of the postwar-designed amphibious tractors to enter marine service was the 43-ton LVTH6. Like the LVTA5, the LVTH6 served not as an amphibious troop transport vehicle, but rather as a fire-support vehicle with its turret-armed 105mm howitzer. Pictured firing at enemy positions in support of marine infantrymen during the Vietnam War is a LVTH6. While it looked much like a tank, the vehicle's steel armor was only 1/4-inch at its thickest point. National Archives

The beginning of the Korean War sparked an interest by the marines in the development of a new family of LVTs that would serve several different roles and be based on the same chassis. The first member of this family rolled off the production line in August 1951 and was assigned the designation LVTH6 (H for howitzer). The massive, barge-like vehicle was delivered with a turret-mounted 105mm howitzer. The 43-ton LVTH6 also featured a coaxial .30-caliber M1919A4E1 machine gun and an M2 .50-caliber machine gun that could be mounted on the turret's roof.

generation LVTs. Except for those units already deployed overseas, only the newest LVT versions remained in service. These included the 15-ton LVT3 and the 20-ton LVTA5 (A for armored). Both vehicle types were upgraded in the postwar era. The LVT3 became the LVTC3, and the LVTA5 became the LVTA5 (Modified).

Shown crossing a South Vietnamese river in March 1968 during Operation Saline II is a Marine Corps LVTP5. As was typical during the Vietnam War, the passengers rode on top of the vehicle for fear of being inside the vehicle if it ran over a mine. The LVTP5 came with a small machine-gun-armed turret on top of the vehicle hull. Because of its location, the gun could not cover a lot of space around the vehicle, so the marines assigned to the vehicle built a small sandbag bunker on the front of the vehicle's hull. National Archives

Pictured on display at the Marine Corps Amphibious Tractor Museum at Camp Pendleton in Southern California is a roughly 20-ton LVTA5 Modified. Unlike other LVTs designed strictly as amphibious troop transport, the LVTA5 was a fire-support vehicle and was armed with a power-operated turret that contained a 75mm howitzer. The vehicle was also armed with a several machine guns. Michael Green

The LVTH6's mission role was to provide fire support during beach assaults for the infantry personnel carrier version of the vehicle designated the LVTP5 (*P* for personnel carrier). The 43-ton vehicle had a three-man crew and could transport up to 25 marines from ship to shore or up to 35 passengers on land. Armament of the LVTP5 consisted of a small, one-man turret armed with a flex-mounted M1919A4 .30-caliber machine gun.

To recover disabled LVTP5s or LVTH6s, a recovery version of the vehicle was designated LVTR1 (*R* for recovery). To breach obstacles and clear paths through minefields during amphibious assault operations, the corps also fielded the LVTE1 (*E* for engineer). The engineer variant had a very large full-width mine plow on the front of the vehicle. All four variants of the LVT saw extensive use with the corps during the Vietnam War. Like all their amtrac predecessors, these vehicles were powered in the water by their paddle-like tracks.

Post-Vietnam War Amphibious Tractors

The marines' dissatisfaction with the unreliable and mechanically complex LVTH6, LVTP5, LVTR1, and LVTE 1 caused them to look for a replacement family of vehicles. In 1965, FMC Corporation was contracted to design and build a new family of LVTs for the corps. FMC had built thousands of LVTs for the marines during World War II and had a great deal of experience in their design and construction. The marines received the first of 15 pre-production prototype vehicles from FMC in 1967. Testing of these vehicles continued until 1969. Rather than being built

Round headlight wells mark the LVTP7 pictured as being from the original production run of the vehicle. The prototypes for this vehicle featured a small turret operated by the vehicle commander that was armed with an M139 20mm automatic cannon and an M73E1 7.62mm machine gun. Unfortunately, funding and operational issues caused the corps to use a single turret-mounted M85 .50-caliber machine gun as an interim measure until the issues with the 20mm automatic-cannon-armed turret resolved themselves, which they never did. Defense Visual Information Center

Pictured on a white sandy beach are a couple of marine LVTP7s. The onboard infantry has taken up defensive positions around the vehicles. The LVTP7 and all its successors are 26 feet long, 10 feet 7 inches wide (without any extra armor added), and about 10 feet high. The vehicle's engine sits in the forward part of the hull and is removable for servicing. Defense Visual Information Center

Taken during a training exercise in Norway is this picture of a line of camouflaged Marine Corps LVTP7s. Compared to the box-like hull of the LVTP5, the LVTP7 had a more boat-like appearance with a very narrow front hull that sharply tapered back into an angled lower front hull. TheLVTP7 had a crew of three men, a vehicle commander, a driver, and an assistant driver. The vehicle's rear hull had room for 25 lightly equipped marine infantry-men. Defense Visual Information Center

of thin steel armor plate as the LVTH6, LVTP5, LVTR1, and LVTE-1 had been, the hulls for the new family of amphibious tractors were fabricated from aluminum alloy armor.

The corps was very impressed with FMC's prototype vehicles and soon placed an order for 1,081 production vehicles. Three different variants rolled off the factory floor between 1970 and 1974. The most numerous was the personnel carrier version designated the LVTP7, of which 942 were built. There were also 84 command post variants (designated the LVTC7) and 55 recovery variants (designated the LVTR7). The LVTR7 came with a crane, winches, and other special machinery to rescue stranded vehicles and make major repairs to return them to service.

Each LVT7-series vehicle weighed about 25 tons and was powered by General Motors liquid-cooled eight-cylinder diesel engines with a top speed of 40 miles per hour on level ground. The semiautomatic transmission had four forward and two reverse speeds while in land mode. In water mode, two water-jet propulsion units at the rear of each vehicle propelled it to a top speed of about 8 knots. The water jets were connected to the vehicle's transmission by drive shafts that ran the length of the vehicle. A pair of power take-offs on the transmission drove the jets at an efficient speed for water propulsion. In water mode, the driver's steering wheel moved deflectors into the output stream, which changed the stream's direction for steering. The electrically operated deflectors were large scoops mounted directly behind each of the two water jets.

The water-jet propulsion system mounted on the LVT7 and all subsequent versions of the vehicle work on jet reaction principles, which are similar to the way jet aircraft engines work, except that the operating medium is water instead of air. Water is channeled into the water-jet inlets through two inlet ducts near the center of the vehicle's hull. Water jets are specialized pumps that increase the speed of the water as it passes through them. This fast-moving water then goes into outlet nozzles that adjust the output stream to produce the maximum thrust for efficient water propulsion. The combination of water-jet pumps and steering deflectors resulted in a simple, efficient, and controllable water-propulsion system for the entire LVT7 series. This water propulsion system is still in use today.

When the LVT7 series was originally designed, the Marine Corps' primary mission was to ferry troops and cargo from ship to shore and back again. By the late 1970s, the corps began to realize that its LVT7s were spending the majority of their time on land as armored personnel carriers. In January 1979, the corps reflected this change in the vehicle's mission profile by renaming it the amphibious assault vehicle (AAV) series rather than the long-standing designation of landing vehicle tracked (LVT). Hence, the troop-carrier version of the LVTP7 became the AAVP7, the command version became the AAVC7, and the recovery version became the AAVR7.

In the early 1980s the Marine Corps contracted with FMC to upgrade the entire AAV7 series of vehicles in its inventory under a service life extension program (SLEP). Among the upgrade features was the fitting of the Cummins eight-cylinder, multi-fuel, diesel engine used in the Bradley fighting vehicle family. The higher power of this engine pushed the vehicle's top speed on land to 45 miles per hour. Reflecting the many changes to the vehicle design, the corps designated all the rebuilt AAV7s as AAV7A1s. In addition to the SLEP program for its older vehicles, the corps awarded FMC a contract to build 333 new AAV7A1s. These included 294 new personnel carriers, 29 command vehicles, and 10 recovery vehicles.

The original LVTP7's armament consisted of an M85 .50-caliber machine gun mounted in a small, one-man, electric-hydraulic turret. The turret was occupied by the vehicle's commander and could be traversed manually if the need arose. The LVTC7 and LVTR7 had no armament fitted. With the introduction of the AAVP7A1, a new, all-electric-powered turret was installed on the vehicle. It remained armed, however, with the same M85 .50-caliber machine gun as found on the original LVTP7 turret.

In an effort to improve the firepower of its inventory of AAVP7A1s, the marines awarded a contract to Cadillac Gage Corporation to supply 340 turrets mounting Mk.19 40mm automatic grenade launchers and coaxial M2 .50-caliber machine guns. The marines later ordered another 813 of these turrets from AV Technology to bring the remaining AAVP7A1s up to the new armament standard.

The basic hull of the AAV7A1 family of vehicles can defeat only small-arm fire and artillery fragments. To add an improved degree of protection, the marines began to explore adding extra exterior armor to the AAV7A1s in the early 1980s. It wasn't until 1987 that the corps was able to award a contract for the manufacture of 189 kits of add-on armor called the P-900 appliqué armor kit (AAK). The kit consisted of two layers of flat perforated steel armor plates attached to the sides of the AAV7A1 hull and was capable of defeating 14.5mm machine-gun fire. While the AAKs came from a U.S. factory, they were designed by an Israeli firm.

Very impressed with the potential of the AAK, the corps ordered 1,317 improved kits in 1989. The improved version received the name enhanced appliqué armor kit (EAAK), he last of which arrived in 1993. It consisted of two layers of steel alloy armor with a variety of non-metallic materials sandwiched between them. Unlike the earlier AAK that consisted of only flat armor plates, the EAAK fit the contours of the vehicle's hull. The EAAK also provided protection to the hull roof and roof hatches of the AAV7A1. Spall liners on the interior of the hull are also part of the EAAK package. The new armor protects against 14.5mm machine gun fire and 152mm artillery fragments. The added weight of the appliqué armor and the other improvements made since the introduction of the original LVTP7 have pushed the AAVP7A1 variant's weight over 28 tons.

Like all machines subjected to hard use, the marine's fleet of AAV7A1s began to wear out by the late 1990s. To correct this situation, the corps funded a complete overhaul of most of its AAV7A1-series fleet in 2000. During the overhaul, the older major components were swapped for those used in the latest versions of the army's Bradley fighting vehicles. They include the Bradley's 525 horsepower engine/transmission and suspension, including the track. The program is called reliability and maintainability/rebuild to standards (RAM/RS) and was completed in 2003.

The Bradley suspension system on the RAM/RS AAV7A1-series vehicles has increased ground clearance from just 12 to 16 inches. Like the new suspension, the extra 4 inches of ground clearance is almost impossible to discern from a distance. The only external feature that allows a novice to distinguish the upgraded from the non-upgraded AAV7A1s is the relocation of the engine exhaust and muffler from directly behind the engine compartment to directly behind the vehicle commander's cupola.

Crew & Passenger Positions

The AAVP7A1 has a three-man crew consisting of a driver, an assistant driver, and a vehicle commander who communicate with each other through an intercom system using headphones and microphones built into their helmets. The driver of the AAVP7A1 sits at the front of the vehicle to the left of the engine compartment. With his armored hatch closed, the driver looks through seven vision blocks in the cupola. The driver also has a thermal driver's sight.

The vehicle commander of the AAVP7A1 sits on the right front of the vehicle's hull opposite the engine compartment, which is to his left. He sits underneath the armed turret that turns on a bearing mounted to the top of the vehicle's hull. With his overhead turret hatch closed, the vehicle commander views the terrain outside the vehicle through one of several vision blocks.

The assistant driver is the crew's junior marine in the crew. His position is in the left rear seat in the troop compartment near the large ramp at the back of the vehicle. In the water, he scans the interior for leaks and is ready to help the embarked infantry if an evacuation is needed. On land, he helps the infantry enter and exit the vehicle and lets the vehicle commander know when the ramp is clear so that it can be raised.

The rear of the hull is the passenger compartment of the AAVP7A1. Typically, 16 to 18 marine infantry troops sit on three long bench seats in the passenger compartment. The squad leader is stationed in a seat just behind the driver. The troops consist of a rifle squad of 13 marines reinforced with elements of the infantry company's weapons platoon, which is a mix of machine gun, mortar, and antitank teams.

When the squad leader closes his overhead hatch, he looks through seven vision blocks in his cupola. The

In 1983 the Marine Corps received its first production example of an upgraded LVTP7 designated the assault amphibious vehicle-7A1 (AAVP7A1). A distinguishing outside feature of the AAVP7A1 and of the command-and-recovery versions of that vehicle were the square headlight wells seen on the vehicle pictured. Other changes included raising the squad leader's cupola, which is located just behind the driver position, 8 inches. Defense Visual Information Center

Dissatisfaction with the turret armament on the LVTP7 and the AAVP7A1, which consisted of only a single M85 .50-caliber machine gun led the Marine Corps to consider mounting a new up-armed turret on their fleet of AAVP7A1s. What eventually appeared was a new power-operated turret that mounted a Mk. 19 40mm automatic grenade launcher and a coaxial M2 .50-caliber machine gun as seen in this picture. Greg Stewart

A serious problem that has long plagued the Marine Corps' fleet of AAV7s has been the vehicle's very thin armor. To correct this, the Marine Corps sought a suitable appliqué armor kit for its vehicles. Pictured coming out of the surf is an AAVP7A1 featuring a P900 appliqué armor kit (AAK). The corps acquired only 189 examples of the AAK, none of which remain in service today. Greg Stewart

Seen here mounted on an AAVP7A1 (RAM/RS) is the enhanced appliqué armor kit (EAAK) that the corps adopted after testing the P-900 AAK. The Marine Corps ordered over 1,000 examples of the EAAK. Since their delivery in the early 1990s, the number of EAAKs has declined due to serious rust damage. Many AAV7A1 vehicles that participated in Operation Iraqi Freedom were not fitted with EAAKs. Michael Green

Two Marine Corps AAVP7A1 (RAM/RS) are pictured parked on either side of a road as an enemy truck loaded with 120mm mortar ammunition explodes during Operation Iraqi Freedom. Both vehicles feature only the forward part of the standard EAAK. Along the hull sides of both vehicles, large steel plates of unknown thickness are used instead of the EAAK. The number of marine vehicles that featured this change is unknown. Corporal Mace M. Gratz

squad leader's cupola is a foot higher than the driver's to enable him to see over the front of the vehicle. The armored periscope at the front of his cupola is even higher. Unlike the commander's turret, the squad leader's cupola does not rotate.

Marine infantrymen ride into combat in the AAVP7A1 enter and leave the vehicle through an armored rear access ramp. The ramp raises and lowers with a hydraulically powered control system operated from inside the vehicle. A small armored door in the rear access ramp is used when the vehicle's engine is not running or for emergency egress if the ramp is damaged or disabled. To load cargo, the vehicle has two long overhead cargo hatches that run the length of the crew compartment. On land, the overhead hatches can remain open if the infantrymen need to fire their own small arms over the sides of the vehicle as battlefield conditions dictate.

Fire has always been a major threat to ground-vehicle crews or passengers. An enemy antitank weapon that penetrates the hull or turret of a vehicle can ignite the fuel or flammable items inside the vehicle. If sensors detect fire, the AAVP7A1's advanced Halon 1301 fire-suppression system reacts in milliseconds to extinguish the fire before the crew or passengers can be harmed.

AAV Organization

Twelve AAVP7A1s comprise a platoon. Each platoon can move a reinforced infantry company of 200 marines from ship to shore, or shore to ship, in one mass movement. Platoons are further subdivided into four sections of three vehicles each. An amphibious assault (AA) company has three platoons of AAVs, a headquarters platoon that carries the support staff, and a maintenance platoon.

Two AAVC7A1 dedicated-command vehicles provide protection for the AA company's support-staff vehicles. In addition to its three-man crew, the AAVC7A1s carry a varying number of radio operators and staff officers whose job is to direct the battalion's operations by radio.

The AA company's maintenance platoon is equipped with an AAVR7A1 recovery vehicle, crewed by three men.

Visible in this picture taken inside a marine AAVP7A1 (RAM/RS) is the driver's position. The seat behind the driver's position is for the squad leader. Due to the RAM/RS upgrade program, the modified vehicles have faster acceleration and better mobility over a greater variety of ground than the unmodified vehicles. Michael Green

The rear-hull troop compartment of a marine AAVP7A1 (RAM/RS) is visible in this picture. The infantrymen that operate from this area arrange themselves on three rows of removable bench seats. The center bench-seat section in this picture is temporary attached to the left wall of the hull compartment. Riding inside the vehicle during rough seas is a miserable experience that no marine ever forgets. Michael Green

Visible on the exterior of this marine AAVP7A1 (RAM/RS) are the mounting studs for the EAAK not fitted on the vehicle pictured. Due to vehicle's close quarters, passengers store their duffel bags and sleeping bags on the exterior of the vehicle's hull. The engines on the upgraded RAM/RS vehicles feature new step-time-control injectors that offer better fuel economy, produce less pollution and smoke, and add longer life to parts compared with the unmodified AAV7A1 series vehicles. Michael Green

Marine infantrymen assigned to the Twenty-fourth MEU race out of marine armament carriers down the hydraulically operated rear ramp of an AAVP7A1 (RAM/RS) to take part in a live-fire training exercise. If the rear ramp fails to operate properly, the vehicle's passengers can enter and leave the vehicle through an integral personnel door located in the ramp itself. Photographer's Mate 2nd Class Michael Sandberg

The AAVR7A1 has a very powerful winch as well as a large hydraulic crane with an extending boom capable of changing entire power packs. While numbers sometimes vary among units, the typical AA company fields 47 vehicles.

When AA companies combine, they form amphibious assault (AA) battalions, the composition of which varies in the corps. While one battalion may have four AA companies and a headquarters and service (H&S) company, another may have five AA companies and an H&S company. In the Marine Corps Reserve, AA battalions comprise only two companies plus an H&S company.

A picture from Operation Iraqi Freedom shows the rear of a marine Corps AAVP7A1 not yet upgraded under the RAM/RS program. This is evident since it lacks the engine exhaust and muffler mounted directly behind the vehicle commander's cupola. Also seen in this photograph is one of the two hull compartment overhead hatches and the smoke-grenade launchers mounted on the rear of the vehicle commander's weapon-armed turret. The integral personnel door set into the rear ramp of the vehicle is also visible. Staff Sergeant Bryan P. Reed

The corps lost both men and equipment during Operation Iraqi Freedom. Winched onto an army recovery trailer by marines of Combat Service Support Brigade 18 is a destroyed Marine Corps AAV7A1. Despite the U.S. military's best efforts at preventing friendly fire incidents, some vehicle losses during Iraqi Freedom could be attributed to that cause. What led to the destruction of the vehicle shown is unknown. Master Sergeant Edward D. Kniety

A picture taken from the rear deck of a naval ship shows an overhead view of a marine AAVC7A1. The command variant of both the original LVT7 series, as well as all subsequent versions, lacks the weapon-armed turret seen on the personnel-carrier variants. Instead, they have a fixed cupola for the vehicle command. Clearly seen in this picture are the vehicle's two overhead rear cargo hatches, a feature found on all AAVs. Defense Visual Information Center

Another type of battalion in the corps is the combat assault battalion, which has several different types of units, including one AA company. In the H&S companies of the pure AA battalion, larger communications and maintenance platoons have more AAVC7A1s and AAVR7A1s.

Some AA battalions also have mobility/counter-mobility platoons in their H&S companies. These platoons consist of 24 AAVP7A1s that support combat engineers in clearing minefields and obstacle belts ashore. Half the platoon vehicles contain a rocket system that pulls a line charge—a 100-yard-long belt of explosives—forward of the AAV. These detonate in front of the vehicle to clear a pathway through minefields and light obstacles, and line-charge vehicles can carry three such charges. The other vehicles in the mobility/counter-mobility platoon carry combat engineers who handle more difficult obstacles and mark the paths through the minefields.

Despite the many upgrades made to the corps' current inventory of AAV7A1-series vehicles, they remain a 1960s-era design and are much older than the crews that operate them. When originally fielded by the marines in the early 1970s, the vehicles were intended to be in service for only about 10 years, by which time the corps had hoped to have their light armored vehicle (LAV) in

Pictured at the Marine Corps Amphibious Vehicle Test Branch at Camp Pendleton in Southern California is one of two early prototypes of the advance amphibious assault vehicle (AAAV), now known as the expeditionary fighting vehicle (EFV). It is the intended replacement for the corps' existing fleet of AAV7A1 and AAV7A1 RAM/RS vehicles. The two-man stabilized turret on the EFV is armed with a 30mm high-velocity automatic cannon and coaxial M240 7.62mm machine gun. Michael Green

In the late 1960s, the Marine Corps asked FMC to design an engineer variant for their future LVT7 series of vehicles to be designated the LVTE7. Plans called for a bulldozer blade at the front hull and a mine-clearing-line-charge (MICLIC) kit mounted in the rear hull compartment. The vehicle did not enter production. Instead, the marines adopted a portable MICLIC kit, which could be mounted inside a personnel carrier variant when needed. In this picture the rocket-propelled line charges appear in their launching position. Michael Green

Pictured is the recovery version of the AAV7A1 series, designated the AAVR7A1 RAM/RS. Like the command version, it lacks the weapon-armed turret seen on the personnel-carrier variant. Mounted on the roof of the vehicle is a hydraulic crane with an extended boom that elevates from zero to plus 65 degrees. It also has a recovery winch seen mounted on the nose of the vehicle's hull. Michael Green

service. The LAV program was technologically ambitious and had high projected acquisition and support costs. Early development work showed that the mission effectiveness of the new vehicle would be only slightly greater than existing vehicles, and the program was cancelled in 1985.

In 1989, the corps again made plans to replace its existing AAV7A1 series of vehicles. The new vehicle series was to be called the advanced amphibious assault vehicle (AAAV). Compared to the existing AAV7A1s, it was to have a very high water speed, improved armor protection and more firepower. The marines awarded GDLS the contract to develop and test three prototypes of the future AAAV in 1996. They then awarded GDLS another contract in 2000 to build and test nine more prototypes of the AAAV. If the testing process goes well during the next few years, the corps wants to award GDLS a low-rate production contract in 2006 to build 97 AAAVs. In September of 2003, the corps changed the name of the vehicle from the AAAV to the expeditionary fighting vehicle, (EFV).

If the first 97 examples of the production EFV perform well in the field during testing and training exercises, the corps will award GDLS a full-rate production contract for 1,013 vehicles by 2008. Including the first 90 low-rate production examples of the EFV, the total contract order for GDLS will consist of 935 EFV(P) personnel carrier versions and 78 EFV(C) command vehicles. The personnel carrier version of the EFV(P) will have a three-man crew consisting of a vehicle commander, a gunner, and a driver. It will be able to carry up to 17 fully equipped marine infantrymen.

The current fleet of AAV7A1s has a top water speed of only 8 knots—not much faster than their World War II predecessors. To move much faster, they would need to rise to the surface so they could skim (plane) the waves like a speedboat. Planing requires a large amount of power, a special hydrodynamic hull design, and movable covers for the suspension. This requires a totally new vehicle configuration.

The 37-ton (combat loaded) EFV tracked suspension system can be withdrawn into the sponson area as the vehicle enters the water. Simultaneously, three sets of appendages are deployed in the front, rear, and bottom. These mechanisms streamline the hull bottom and reduce drag to a minimum. The high power and flat, smooth bottom of the EFV allow it to rise to the surface and plane like a speedboat.

The EFV is required to go between 20 and 25 knots in the water. To accomplish this feat, the vehicle has a 12-cylinder, DaimlerChrysler MTU, water-cooled, 2,700 horsepower, turbocharged, diesel engine that drives the vehicle's two large, rear-mounted, 23 inch water-jet propulsion system units. When operating in shallow rivers or in areas with sandbars, the EFV suspension is in the down position. As a result, the EFV plows through the water at 8 knots like AAVs before it. The suspension remains exposed to prevent damage if it encounters shallow spots or strikes a submerged object.

On land, the 2,700 horsepower EFV diesel engine is held to a maximum of 850 horsepower to prevent damage to the transmission and other components. The EFV can

This very impressive picture shows the moment at which the explosive charges attached to cables from an MICLIC kit installed on the Marine Corps AAVP7A1 in the foreground have exploded over a minefield. A Marine Corps M1A1 common tank is pictured leading the way for the more lightly armored AAVP7A1 that is carrying the MICLIC kit. The MICLIC will clear a path through an enemy minefield about 40 feet wide and 300 feet long. Defense Visual Information Center

are lined with Kevlar, which protects the crew and passengers from spalling if the vehicle is hit. There are currently no plans to fit an armor array on the EFV (P) that will defeat shape-charge warheads.

The EFV (P) has a two-man turret armed with a 30mm Mk. 44 Bushmaster automatic cannon and a coaxial M240 7.62mm machine gun. The Bushmaster cannon can destroy a variety of enemy armored vehicles, but not tanks. The EFV weapons and their sights are fully stabilized. This allows the EFV crew to accurately aim the guns and engage targets even while the vehicle is moving. The gunner has a forward looking infrared (FLIR) system and a laser range finder so he can operate the guns at night or in poor weather conditions.

The EFV(C) command variant features a cupola in place of the weapon-armed turret seen on the EFV (P). In addition, the entire roof area over the rear hull compartment has been raised to allow for the placement of seven command-and-control computer workstations inside the crew compartment. Like the EFV (P), the EFV (C) will also carry VHF radios and satellite communication devices.

reach a top speed of 45 miles per hour on level roads. It can also cross an 8 foot trench and climb over a 3 foot vertical wall. The maximum operational range on land is about 400 miles.

The hull of the EFV-series vehicles can defeat 14.5mm armor-piercing rounds. Inside the vehicle, the crew and passengers sit on mine-blast proof seats. Interior walls

Taken from a helicopter is this picture showing a prototype EFV running on the open ocean at high speed. Using a planing hull concept, much like a recreational boat, the EFV can reach speeds of over 20 knots. The result is a vehicle that can be safely launched from far out at sea and cross miles of open ocean in minutes instead of the hours it would take with existing amphibious vehicles that are restricted to a top water speed of about 6 knots. U.S. Marine Corps

AERIAL WEAPONS SYSTEMS

Pictured is an example of the famous gull-wing F4U Corsair fighter landing on a U.S. Navy aircraft carrier during World War II. Between 1942 and 1952 American factories built over 12,000 Corsairs in a variety of versions. During the Korean War the Corsair specialized in low-altitude missions in support of Marine ground combat units. National Archives

The birth of Marine Corps aviation occurred on May 22, 1912, when Marine Corps First Lieutenant Alfred A. Cunningham reported for flight training with the navy. When the United States officially entered World War I in 1917, the corps' First Aviation Force had grown to four squadrons. By July 1918, the force had deployed to northern France under navy control. Instead of supporting Marine Corps ground forces in France, they conducted attacks on German submarines in the English Channel and German sub bases at Ostend, Zeebrugge, and Bruges.

The First Aviation Force used British-designed DH-4 Liberty planes, better known as the De Havilland 4. During World War I, the marines also deployed the first marine aeronautic company, which was equipped with seaplanes to conduct antisubmarine patrols in the Atlantic Ocean.

In the years that followed the World War I marine aviators saw combat in the skies over the Caribbean and Central America in a series of small-scale brush wars. Between the wars, marine pilots began to experiment with the ground-attack tactics they would use to good effect in World War II. They flew Douglas DT-2 torpedo-bombers, Boeing PW-9/FB-1 pursuit planes (fighters), Curtiss F8C-4 Helldiver dive bombers, and a few other aircraft.

World War II marine aircraft included the Brewster F2A-2 Buffalo armed with up to four internally mounted M2 .50-caliber air-cooled machine guns. The Buffalo was clearly obsolete compared to first-line Japanese fighter planes and was replaced in navy and marine service by the Grumman F4F Wildcat. Armed with up to six wing-mounted M2 .50-caliber, air-cooled machine guns, the Wildcat remained a front-line aircraft until the advent of the superior Grumman F6F Hellcat in late 1943. Like the Wildcat, the Hellcat had six wing-mounted M2 .50-caliber machine guns and provisions for carrying bombs and launching rockets.

The famous gullwinged Vought F4U Corsair (also built by other manufactures) supplemented the Hellcat in marine service is World War II. Armed with six wing-mounted M2 .50-caliber machine guns, the Corsair could both carry bombs and launch rockets using its under-wing mounts. One variant of the Corsair came armed with four wing-mounted M3 20mm automatic cannons. While the Wildcat and Hellcat would not survive long in marine service after World War II, the Corsair remained through the Korean War.

The Grumman F7F Tigercat fighter entered marine service late in World War II but didn't see combat action until the Korean War. The Tigercat was armed with up to four internally mounted M2 .50-caliber machine guns and four internally mounted M3 20mm automatic cannons designed by the French firm Hispano-Suiza. The M3's top rate of fire was 750 rounds per minute. The Tigercat also had provisions to mount a variety of bombs, rockets, and even torpedoes underneath the aircraft. Unlike other fighters used by the marines in World War II, the Tigercat had two engines.

Jet-powered combat aircraft that served the corps in Korea War included the McDonnell F2H Banshee, the Grumman F9F Panther and Cougar, as well as the Douglas F3D Skyknight. All these jet-powered subsonic aircraft came armed with four internally mounted M3 20mm automatic cannons and had under-wing pylons for carrying a variety of bombs and rockets.

During the Vietnam War, the marines used a new crop of combat jet aircraft which included the subsonic Douglas A-4 Skyhawk, the supersonic McDonnell Douglas F-4 Phantom II, and the subsonic Grumman A-6 Intruder. The Skyhawk was a light-attack aircraft originally developed in the 1950s. The standard configuration in corps service included two internally mounted Mk. 12 20mm automatic cannons. The weapons could fire 1,000 rounds per minute and evolved from work conducted on a proposed navy shipboard 20mm antiaircraft gun during World War II.

Another antiaircraft weapon that could be mounted on the Skyhawk was the AIM-9 Sidewinder air-to-air, heat-seeking missile. The original version of the Sidewinder entered U.S. military service in 1956. The 200-pound missile is 9 feet long and has a diameter of only 5 inches. The maximum effective range of the latest-version Sidewinder is 11 miles. The Skyhawk also carried a variety of under-wing ordnance.

Two engines powered the McDonnell Douglas F-4 Phantom II, providing a margin of safety not found in the single-engine Skyhawk. Early versions of the Phantom II carried no internally mounted automatic cannon. Instead, an external centerline pod containing a single six-barrel, General Electric M61, 20mm automatic cannon capable of firing 6,000 rounds per minute was sometimes mounted.

Seen on an airfield in South Korea during the Korean War are two Marine Corps Grumman F9F Panthers undergoing refueling. The Panther served with the corps from the late 1940s through the Korean War. Over half of the missions flown by Panthers during the Korean War involved ground-attack missions. The aircraft had four integral M2 20mm automatic cannons and could carry an under-wing ordnance load of almost a ton. National Archives

Pictured is a Rockwell International OV-10A Bronco. The aircraft came out of a tri-service program with the navy, air force, and marine all playing a part in its design and fielding. The Bronco could perform many different roles, including forward air control (FAC), armed reconnaissance, helicopter escort, as well as limited ground attack. Armament on the OV-10A could consist of up to four M60C 7.62mm machine guns plus 3,600 pounds of under-wing ordnance. Defense Visual Information Center

This was a significant increase in firing rate at the time. However, at this rate of fire, the 1,000 or so rounds carried aboard most combat aircraft would be exhausted in a single burst. Because of this, U.S. pilots received training in firing their M61 automatic cannons in short bursts to conserve the aircraft's onboard ammunition.

The M61 cannon first entered U.S. military service in 1956. Development of the weapon was entrusted to General Electric's Armament Division under the code name Vulcan, after the Roman god of fire and metalworking So, the M61 and its descendents are often identified as Vulcan guns. An improved version designated the M61A1 eventually replaced the original version

The Phantom II carried other weapons to supplement the M61's firepower. They included the short-range, air-to-air Sidewinder antiaircraft missile and the longer-ranged, semi-active, radar-homing, Sparrow air-to-air antiaircraft missile. With a maximum effective range of 25 miles, the Sparrow weighs 500 pounds, is 12 feet long, and has an 8-inch diameter body. It first entered marine service in 1965. The Phantom II could carry an impressive variety of under-wing ordnance ranging from bombs to guided missiles. The maximum external load on the aircraft being about 17,000 pounds.

Entering marine service in 1965, the twin-engine Grumman A-6 Intruder was designed for all-weather, subsonic air attacks. In this role, it provided accurate ordnance delivery in day or night. The Intruder's highly capable navigation and ordnance-delivery system allowed for long-range attacks on heavily defended targets. A typical Intruder under-wing load might have included 18 500-pound bombs, eight 1,000-pound bombs, or four 2,000-pound bombs. The Intruder could also carry at least two nuclear weapons but lacked self-defense weapons and depended on supporting aircraft for protection from enemy aircraft.

A prop-driven, single-engine, ground-attack aircraft also in marine service in Korea and Vietnam was the Douglas A1 Skyraider. Exact Skyraider armament

depended on the version used. The corps ground-attack version was usually armed with four wing-mounted M3 20mm automatic cannons and 15 under-wing pylons for carrying either fuel tanks or various types of ordnance.

Another prop-driven marine aircraft used from Vietnam until the early 1990s was the OV-10 Bronco. A twin-engine, multi-purpose, observation-and-reconnaissance aircraft, the Bronco had a crew of two. It could carry an assortment of light rockets and bombs as well as add-on machine-gun pods. It could also mount an air-to-air heat-seeking missile for protection from enemy aircraft.

A Marine Corps F/A-18C assigned to the Red Devils of Marine Fighter Attack Squadron 232 (VMFA-232) continues on its mission after taking fuel from an air force KC-135 Stratotanker in the skies over Iraq during Operation Iraqi Freedom in 2003. The aircraft picture is armed with AIM-9L Sidewinder all-angle, heat-seeking, antiaircraft missiles on both wing tips as well as AGM-88 HARM anti-radar missiles. *Staff Sergeant Cherie A. Thurlby*

THE F/A-18 HORNET

Pictured flying over the Pacific is a marine F/A-18D Hornet. The two-seat D version sees use by the corps and the navy for crew training and the night attack role once performed by the Grumman A-6E Intruder. On the bottom of the fuselage of the aircraft pictured is a painted-on second canopy. Its intended purpose was to confuse enemy pilots as to the true orientation of the Hornet in flight. Hans Halberstadt

By the time of Operation Desert Storm in 1991, the corps had long since retired the prop-driven *Skyraider*. A much-improved version, the A-4M remained in service until the early 1990s, but it was not used in the first Gulf conflict. Desert Storm also proved to be the swan song of the aging Intruder, which, like the Skyhawk, disappeared from corps service in the early 1990s.

The supersonic, twin-engine F/A-18A Hornet entered corps service in the early 1980s and replaced the Phantom II. The prefix F/A identifies the aircraft as a fighter plane as well as a ground-attack aircraft. In the navy and the marine corps, the F/A-18A Hornet was known simply as the F-18. The F/A-18B, a two-seat variant of the Hornet used mainly for training pilots, entered service simultaneously with the F/A-18A. Neither aircraft could conduct night-attack operations.

The twin-engine Hornet can carry the full range of modern U.S. military air-to-air and air-to-ground ordnance. For self-protection, the Hornet has an internally mounted 20mm M61A1 automatic cannon and mounting positions for four air-to-air antiaircraft missiles. The newest versions of the Hornet usually carry two heat-seeking Sidewinder antiaircraft missiles and two 12-foot-long, radar-homing, AIM-120, advanced medium range antiaircraft missiles (AMRAAMs). Nicknamed Slammers, the missiles can strike hostile targets at a range of almost 62 miles and travel at a speed of 2,800 miles per hour. The 340-pound Slammer replaced the Sparrow air-to-air antiaircraft missile.

Since its entering corps service in the early 1980s, the Hornet has been continually upgraded to improve all aspects of its performance. In the late 1980s, the corps

introduced two new versions of the Hornet capable of conducting nighttime attack operations: the single-pilot F/A-18C and the two-person Hornet F/A-18D. The second crewman on the D variant of the Hornet is the weapon system operator (WSO). The addition of a WSO to the D model allowed the Hornet to take over the role once performed by the Intruder, which specialized in nighttime ground attack operations.

During Operation Desert Storm in 1991 and Operation Iraqi Freedom in 2003, the D model performed the role of forward air controller (FAC). As an FAC aircraft, the F/A-18D directed up to 20 other ground-attack aircraft to their assigned targets within a 30-minute time frame. The D version of the Hornet also serves as a training aircraft for the single-seat Hornets, with the installation of a temporary throttle and control stick in the rear seat position of the aircraft. The recent addition of the advanced tactical airborne reconnaissance system (ATARS) to the F/A-18D allows the aircraft to provide marine headquarters with near-real-time, high-resolution digital imagery on the location and strength of enemy forces around the clock, regardless of weather conditions. This intelligence is also available to the other services.

The marines anticipate that the Hornet will remain in service until 2020. Seventy-six early-model F/A-18A Hornets are being cycled through an engineering change program (ECP-583) to bring their combat effectiveness up to modern standards. The ECP program began in 2002 and will continue through 2007. This program provides enhancements to the radar, navigation system, mission computers, communication suite, and night-vision capabilities of the corps' F/A-18A fleet. Aircraft so modified will feature the designation F/A-18A Plus. The corps has a fleet of 168 Hornets of all versions now in service.

Hornet aircraft built after 1991 can achieve top speeds over Mach 1.8, require only 467 yards of runway to take off, and can fly at altitudes over 50,000 feet. When configured as a fighter, with air-to-air antiaircraft missiles fitted, the Hornet's combat radius is about 460 miles. When fully loaded with air-to-ground ordnance, the aircraft's combat radius drops to about 300 miles.

AIR-TO-GROUND WEAPONS OF THE HORNET

Configured as an attack aircraft, the Hornet can carry a wide array of unguided dumb or iron bombs ranging in size from 500 to 2,000 pounds. These are classified general-purpose (GP) bombs and normally contain high explosives. They have either nose (instantaneous) or tail (delay) fuses. Instantaneous fusing is used when maximum blast or fragmentation effect is needed at first impact. A target suitable for an instantaneous fuse is an enemy truck column. A target suitable for a delayed fuse is a runway or road where the bomb can penetrate the surface before exploding for maximum cratering. Some bomb fuses will go off at predetermined altitudes so they'll

Corporal Bridges and Lance Corporal Brown of Marine Aviation Fighter Attack Squadron are pictured loading a Mk. 83 1,000-pound bomb onto an F/A-18 Hornet. The Mk. 83 is just one of dozens of different-sized, unguided, high-explosive dumb or iron bombs in the U.S. military arsenal. Easy and cheap to build in large numbers, they easily convert into guided smart bombs with the addition of various guidance kits that make them extremely accurate. Defense Visual Information Center

explode in the air before the bomb hits the ground. This type of fusing arrangement is very effective against personnel in the open.

For aircraft to be able to drop dumb bombs from altitudes as low as 200 feet, the bombs must be fitted with high-drag fins. The fins slow the bomb's descent so the resulting explosions don't damage the aircraft dropping the bombs. Dumb bombs equipped with high-drag fins are called hi-drag, retarded, or snake-eye bombs.

Another type of dumb bomb carried by the Hornet is the cluster bomb unit (CBU), a large canister that contains smaller, baseball-sized bombs called bomblets or submunitions. Once a pilot drops a CBU canister over an enemy location, the CBU releases the bomblets at a predetermined altitude over the target area to achieve maximum effectiveness. Some bomblets drop to the ground without exploding and use timers to explode later to deny an area to enemy personnel. Bomblet dispensing patterns can be changed to match the shape of the target area attacked.

Small bomblets inside CBUs have an explosive effect similar to a hand grenade or a 60mm mortar round. Their main purpose is to kill or wound exposed enemy troops or to suppress enemy ground-based antiaircraft sites. Some CBUs carry larger bomblets intended to destroy armored and non-armored vehicles; they pack a punch equal to an 81mm mortar round. Another type of CBU carries scatterable mines to slow the advance of an enemy ground force or deny him an area.

A particularly nasty type of unguided air-to-ground ordnance the Hornet can carry is the napalm firebomb. First used in combat by U.S. military aircraft in World War II, napalm can be dropped in close proximity to exposed friendly troops because it produces flames with no blast or fragmentation effect. Napalm firebombs come in different-sized canisters filled with a plasticized fuel called napalm B. A napalm bomb released at low altitude from a high-speed aircraft like the Hornet will typically produce a flame pattern 22 yards wide and 110 yards long.

To increase the accuracy of its dumb bombs, the Hornet has a unit that locks a radar beam onto its intended target and provides data input to a bomb-release computer. The bomb-release computer projects a continuously computed impact point (CCIP) on the pilot's eye-level, heads up display (HUD), showing where the dumb bombs will impact if the pilot pushed the release button on the top of the hands on throttle and stick (HOTAS).

The Hornet is also configured to use smart bombs such as the laser guided bombs (LGBs) called Paveways by the U.S. military. Laser guided bombs are dumb bombs that, when fitted with laser guidance kits, convert to precision-guided bombs within a few minutes. LGBs were introduced into U.S. military service in 1968 during the Vietnam War. They work on a very simple principle. A laser beam from the Hornet, another aircraft, or troops on the ground is aimed at the intended target. The laser paints the target, providing enough illumination for the

A navy officer helps marine ordnance men lift AIM-9 Sidewinder air-to-air antiaircraft missiles off an Aero 21 weapons skid on the flight deck of the amphibious assault ship the USS Tarawa during a training exercise off the coast of Thailand in 1989. Development of the roughly 200-pound missile began in the early 1950s. Continuously upgraded and improved over the decades since it entered service, it remains a potent aerial weapon system today. Defense Visual Information Center

laser-light seeker in the nose cone of every LGB to detect. Immediately after the LGB drops from a Hornet, the laser-light seeker homes in on the target. The tail fins of the Paveway laser guidance kit respond to commands from the laser-light seeker in the nose of the bomb, which allows in-flight trajectory correction while the bomb is en

route to its target. LGBs saw heavy use during Operation Desert Storm.

LGBs have some battlefield disadvantages, including their inability to operate effectively in rain and poor weather. Smoke may also interfere with the LGB's effectiveness. Even in optimum weather, LGBs require a laser-painted target during their entire drop, which makes the launching aircraft a potential target for enemy antiaircraft weapons.

To overcome the battlefield shortcomings of LGBs, the U.S. military has converted to satellite-guided smart bombs. Now, instead of depending on a bomb-carrying aircraft like the Hornet to identify and paint its own targets, troops on the ground, other pilots, or battlefield commanders can radio a set of global positioning system (GPS) coordinates to a patrolling aircraft. After the pilot of the patrolling aircraft enters the number sequences into the onboard fire-control computer, the data is downloaded to a small GPS computer within the smart bomb's add-on guidance and control conversion kit. When the pilot releases the bomb, the onboard navigation system (ONS) in the bomb's guidance and control system uses movable tail fins in the guidance conversion kit to steer it precisely to the GPS coordinates. Target identification and weather conditions are irrelevant, as the pilot may never see the intended target.

GPS-aided weapons were first used in Operation Enduring Freedom, in Afghanistan in 2001. These fire-and-forget weapons played an important role in Operation Iraqi Freedom in 2003. The most common type of GPS-aided bomb carried on the Hornet is the joint direct attack munitions (JDAM) weapon. (The term joint identifies weapons used by the air force, navy, and marines.) When released from an altitude of 20,000 feet, the JDAM has a range of about 8 miles. A future version of the JDAM features a glider attachment that will push its maximum effective range to almost 24 miles.

Another type of GPS-guided bomb carried by the Hornet is the joint standoff weapon (JSOW). The JSOW is a large, specially designed bomb weighing between 1,000 and 1,500 pounds. Wings deploy in flight, allowing it to glide long distances to its intended target. The range of the JSOW is almost 40 miles, depending on the launching altitude. There are different versions of the JSOW, each with a different mission. One model is designed to destroy personnel and other soft targets in the open. Another variant is designed to destroy enemy tanks and other armored fighting vehicles.

The Hornet is also an effective platform for launching air-to-ground missiles. The 13-foot-long, high-speed, anti-radiation missile (AGM-88 HARM) is the most commonly used missile. HARM homes in on electromagnetic signals from enemy radar installations. When the armed missile identifies a radar signal as hostile, HARM alerts the pilot of the aircraft carrying the weapon. Once launched, the 800-pound HARM travels to its target at a speed of over 1,400 miles per hour. The high-explosive warhead weighs about 45 pounds and contains thousands of small steel or tungsten fragments. These hard, sharp fragments are very effective at shredding the antennas of enemy radar systems. The maximum effective range of the weapon is about 30 miles.

THE AV-8B HARRIER II

On the flight deck of a naval ship, a Marine Corps AV-8B Harrier II is pictured taxiing off to its storage position under the guidance of a member of the ship's crew. The original version of the aircraft that entered corps service in the 1970s was designated the AV-8A Harrier. The AV-8B Harrier II was an upgraded version of the AV-8A and began to appear in corps service in 1984. The big improvement to the Harrier II was a much larger wing made of lightweight composite materials and new larger integral fuel tanks that greatly increased the aircraft's operational range.
Defense Visual Information Center

An aircraft unique to the marines in the U.S. armed forces is the single-seat McDonnell Douglas AV-8 Harrier II. (There is also a two-seat trainer version of the aircraft.) Unlike the Hornet, which requires a large paved runway or a carrier deck for launch and recovery, the Harrier II is operable from almost any paved surface larger than a tennis court. This is due to the Harrier's vertical take off and landing (VTOL) capability. The aircraft also has a short take off and vertical landing (STVOL) mode that is easier and safer for pilots to use. The VTOL and STVOL capabilities allow the corps to position Harriers close enough to frontline marines to deliver supporting ordnance in as little as 10 minutes.

Originally based on a British-designed aircraft, the Harrier II has continually evolved in capability and reliability. The first version of the aircraft, which replaced the Skyhawk, entered Marine Corps service in 1971 and bore the designation AV-8A Harrier. Between 1979 and 1984, 47 AV-8A Harriers were upgraded to an AV-8C configuration. A much-improved and more capable second-generation Harrier entered marine service in 1987 with the designation AV-8B Harrier II. This version replaced all earlier A and C model Harriers. There are currently about 110 Harrier IIs in the corps' inventory.

Beginning in 1989, McDonnell Douglas began a conversion program to enable the Harrier II aircraft to fly at night in clear weather. The upgrade included a forward-looking infrared sensor, a color digital moving map, and night-vision goggles for the pilot. The forward-looking IR sensor provided a video image of the scene ahead of the aircraft on the pilot's HUD, which helps the pilot to navigate and identify ground targets. The digital map helps the pilot by displaying navigational, threat, and intelligence information. The pilot uses night-vision goggles designed specifically for nighttime flying to identify and track targets outside the infrared sensor's field of view.

As early as 1987, McDonnell Douglas began the process of upgrading the Harrier II. This effort eventually led to another version upgrade, the Harrier II Plus. The first production example of the Harrier II was put into service in 1993. The upgrade retrofitted the aircraft with the same radar system as the Hornet's, allowing it to fire the AIM-120 Slammer air-to-air antiaircraft missile and the 660 pound, 12 feet 7 inch-long AGM-84 Harpoon all weather, over-the-horizon, antiship missile. The Harpoon has a maximum effective range of almost 40 miles and can also be fired from the Hornet. The top speed of the Harrier

Ready to descent onto the deck of a naval ship is a Marine Corps McDonnell Douglas Night-Attack AV-8B Harrier II. This variant of the aircraft first entered service in 1987. Earlier versions of the aircraft could not operate at night or in poor weather conditions. The small rounded fairing over the nose of the aircraft containing its forward-looking infrared (FLIR) sensor identifies the night-attack version of the Harrier II. Hans Halberstadt

II Plus is 690 miles per hour at sea level.

Because of hard use by the marines, all Harrier II Plus aircraft have been refurbished a second time to extend their service life beyond 2016. At that time, the corps hopes to replace the Harrier II and the Hornet with a version of the Lockheed Martin F-35 joint strike fighter (JSF), a planned family of three very similar aircraft, each configured specifically for the marines, air force, and navy. The air force variant will be the F-35A, marine's will be the F-35B, and the navy's will be the F-35C. The major unique characteristic of the F-35B marine variant will be its STVOL capability brought from the Harrier. Operational testing of the F-35 JSF variants is scheduled to begin in 2010.

The original marine Harrier variant was armed with a British 25mm automatic cannon in a pod attached to the underside of the aircraft's fuselage. All subsequent variants have mounting provisions under the fuselage for a pod that contains a General Electric 25mm GAU-12A five-barrel, Gatling-type, air-powered, automatic cannon called the Equalizer. Three hundred rounds of 25mm

ammunition feed to the gun pod from a companion ammunition pod attached to the underside of the fuselage. The Equalizer's rate of fire varies from 3,600 to 4,200 rounds per minute. The weapon is equally effective in air-to-air or air-to-ground roles.

The Harrier II can also carry most of the ordnance that was formerly mounted on the Hornet. The unguided rockets most commonly mounted on Harriers are 2.75 inch-diameter folding fin aircraft rockets (FFAR) and 5 inch Zuni rockets. Both were originally developed for use during the Vietnam War. The FFAR rockets have an overall length with wings folded of 4 feet and weigh about 21 pounds. They mount either a 9.1-pound high-explosive warhead or a shape-charge antitank warhead. The current Zuni 5 inch rocket is about 6 feet long and weighs 80 pounds. The two most common warheads include one that creates smoke for target marking and incendiary missions and another that functions as a combination antipersonnel and antitank general purpose warhead.

An extremely powerful cluster bomb carried by the Hornet and Harrier II Plus bears the designation fuel-air-

A Marine Corps AV-8B Harrier II (Plus) on the flight deck of a naval ship during Operation Iraqi Freedom in 2003. The plus variant of the Harrier II first entered service in 1993 and features a new APG-65 radar system that allows it to fly night-attack missions in any type of weather with a degree of precision that was unattainable with earlier versions of the aircraft. A visual clue to this version of the Harrier is the box-like fairing over the nose. Staff Sergeant Bryan Reed

explosive (FAE) weapon. Developed for use during the Vietnam War, the current version of the weapon weighs 500 pounds and carries three 100-pound bomblets. Each bomblet contains 75 pounds of ethylene oxide with an air-burst fuse set to go off at an altitude of 30 feet. When the bomblets open, they dispense a large aerosol cloud that hovers just above the ground. Seconds later, an embedded detonator ignites the aerosol cloud and creates a massive explosion and blast wave more powerful than a conventional high-explosive bomb of comparable size. The effects of the blast wave are especially damaging to personnel hiding in bunkers, trench lines, buildings, and other enclosed spaces. The marines used FAE cluster bombs against Iraqi troops in both the first and second wars with that country.

Hornets and Harriers also carry the AGM-65 Maverick—a powerful tank-killing, air-to-surface guided missile. The roughly 700-pound Maverick comes armed with a 230-pound blast-penetrator warhead. The missile is 8 feet 1 inch long and has a diameter of 11.8 inches. It uses either a laser guidance system or a TV seeker to find its targets on the battlefield. As a laser-guided weapon, it bears the designation AGM-65E. When fitted with a TV seeker, it is designated the AGM-65J.

HELICOPTER GUNSHIPS

The Marine Corps received its first helicopters in 1948. They bore the designation HO3S-1 observation-utility helicopters. Built by Sikorsky Aircraft, they were powered by a 450 horsepower gasoline engine and could carry a single pilot and two combat-equipped marine infantrymen. The maximum load of the HO3S-1, including the pilot and passengers, cargo, and fuel was 1,180 pounds. It didn't take long for the marines to discover that a larger helicopter was required. By the time of the Vietnam War, the corps had placed into service a variety of transport helicopters including the massive CH-53A Sea Stallion that could carry 37 passengers or 16,000 pounds of cargo. All of the corps' transport helicopters were soon equipped with a variety of door-mounted machine guns for self-protection.

During the Vietnam War the marines became aware of the army's development of a dedicated helicopter gunship in lieu of modified transport helicopters adapted to the gunship role. When the army fielded the original Bell Helicopter-designed AH-1G Huey Cobra gunship in South Vietnam in late 1967, the marines quickly realized that they needed a similar helicopter for their own requirements. In 1968 they ordered 68 twin-engine variants of the army's helicopter gunship. Designated the AH-1J Sea Cobra, this variant had a two-place, tandem-seat arrangement with the gunner in front and the pilot in a slightly raised rear-seat position similar to the cockpit arrangement of the army's AH-1G Cobra.

In addition to the extra engine (an important feature when operating over water), the *Sea Cobra* boasted a

The first production helicopter in corps service was the Sikorsky HO3S-1 as pictured here during the Korean War. The helicopter is transporting wounded marines to rear area medical-aid stations. A two-man crew, consisting of a pilot and an observer, sat in a large glazed cabin at the front of the helicopter's fuselage. The HO3S-1 helicopter had a normal cruising speed of about 85 miles per hour. National Archives

chin turret at the front of the fuselage, armed with a single M197 20mm automatic gun. The M197 gun is a shortened, three-barrel version of the M61 six-barrel Gatling-type gun carried by most U.S. military fighter aircraft. In theory, the maximum firing rate of the M197 is 3,000 rounds per minute. Since the Sea Cobra can carry only about 700

Belonging to a Marine Corps Helicopter Transport Squadron is a Sikorsky HRS-3. It is pictured dropping off marine infantrymen during a training exercise. The helicopter had a three-man crew consisting of two pilots and a crew chief. It could carry eight passengers at a cruising speed of about 85 miles per hour to an operational range of about 350 miles. Machine guns and rockets could be mounted on the helicopter. National Archives

On the flight deck of a naval ship is an example of a Marine Corps AH-1T Sea Cobra gunship. It lacks the forward-looking infrared (FLIR) sensor mounted on the nose of subsequent versions of the helicopter. Hence, it has a smooth metal fairing over the nose section and a three-barrel M197 20mm Gatling-type automatic cannon mounted directly below it. Defense Visual Information Center

Hovering over the flight deck of a naval ship is a Marine Corps AH-1W Super Cobra. Notice that the FLIR sensor at the nose of the aircraft and above the gun-armed chin turret has changed the helicopter's profile. Many marines call the AH-1W Super Cobra the Whiskey Cobra since the letter *W* in military phonetic code is whiskey. Defense Visual Information Center

Aviation ordnance marines push a small cart containing two 2.75 inch rocket launcher pods and a 5 inch Zuni rocket launcher pod across the flight deck of a naval ship. The pods would be mounted on an AH-1W Super Cobra taking part in Operation Enduring Freedom in Afghanistan in December 2001. The 2.75 inch rockets come with many different types of warheads, including the standard high-explosive antitank with a shape-charge, high-explosive fragmentation and white phosphorus. Staff Sergeant Daniel C. Hottle

rounds, this rate is seldom used. In addition to the M197, the Sea Cobras carried various types of unguided rockets in external under-wing pylons.

Before their Sea Cobras were delivered, the marines obtained 38 AH-1G model Cobras from the army for use in South Vietnam. The marine's Sea Cobras finally arrived in South Vietnam in early 1971 and saw combat during the closing stages of the U.S. involvement in the Vietnam War. The borrowed army AH-1G Cobras eventually ended up in a marine reserve unit, where they spent the remainder of their service life.

Almost immediately after the Sea Cobra entered Marine Corps service, the marines discovered that they needed a helicopter able to carry a greater load of weapons in high-temperature conditions. This resulted in the development of the AH-1T Cobra, tailored for marine missions. In addition to an upgraded engine and transmission, it featured an extended fuselage and tail boom. It also had a larger-diameter rotor to create more lift. These improvements allowed the AH-1T Cobra to carry TOW 2 antitank missile launchers in addition to the rocket pods on its external under-wing pylons. The helicopter's cockpit was protected by ballistic glass able to defeat many types of small arms fire. Both the AH-1T's main rotor and the rear tail boom can defeat automatic cannon fire up to 23mm.

In 1986, another upgrade of the Sea Cobra—the AH-1W Super Cobra—was placed into corps service. The new version featured more powerful engines and advanced electronics adding the capability to fire the Sidewinder air-to-air antiaircraft missile, the AGM-122

A young Marine inserts a 2.75 inch Zuni unguided rocket into a launcher pod mounted on the underside of a stub wing of an AH-1W Super Cobra. The rockets come in an assortment of warheads including high explosive and smoke. Like all airborne unguided rockets, they are for short-range use only when the enemy has no effective antiaircraft defenses. To the left of the rocket-launcher pod are the mounts for the fitted TOW 2 antitank missiles. Corporal Jeff Sisto

On April 13, 2003 during Operation Iraqi Freedom a pair of Marine Corps AH-1W Super Cobras ran short of fuel, which forced them to make an emergency landing on a road just outside Baghdad. Luckily for them, they landed next to a convoy of trucks from Marine Wing Support Squadron 373 moving forward to set up a forward-arming and refueling point. Lance Corporal Nicholous Radloff

During Operation Iraqi Freedom Marine Corporal Alvin Hicks, of Marine Air Wing Support Squadron 373's bulk fuel section, refuels an AH-1W Cobra from the Third Marine Aircraft Wing in a forward-aircraft refueling point at an air base in Iraqi. The Cobra has a full complement of four Hellfire fire-and-forget antitank missiles on the stub-wing visible to the camera, as well as a 5-inch Zuni rocket pod. Lance Corporal C. H. Fitzgerald

Pictured at the Marine Corps Air Ground Combat Center at Twentynine Palms in Southern California is a UH-1N Huey helicopter belonging to the Thirteenth MEU. The mounting brackets for a door-mounted machine gun and a rocket-launcher pod are visible on the right fuselage side of the helicopter. Because of their age, the corps' inventory of UH-1N helicopters will soon be rebuilt and upgraded and will be designated the UH-1Y. Michael Green

Sidearm air-to-ground anti-radiation missile, and the air-to-ground laser-guided AGM-114 Hellfire antitank missile.

The Sidearm anti-radiation missile is a variant of the Sidewinder antiaircraft missile and performs the same basic function as the much larger and heavier HARM anti-radiation missile used on the Hornet. It uses a modified Sidewinder guidance section to detect and track ground-based antiaircraft radar systems. Besides its use on the Super Cobra, it can also be mounted on the Harrier II.

The 100-pound Hellfire is 5 feet long with a diameter of 7 inches. It has a 5-mile range when launched from high altitudes. Typically, helicopter gunships like the Super Cobra tend to fly low to the ground to avoid enemy ground-based antiaircraft weapon systems. At this altitude, the range of weapons like the Hellfire is limited to less than 2 miles. Prior to 1996, the Super Cobras depended on laser designators carried by ground troops or other aircraft to illuminate targets. Super Cobras now carry their own laser designators for engaging targets.

Since military technology is continually advancing, the Marine Corps needs to upgrade its more complex equipment or risk obsolescence. The Super Cobra is now in the first stage of a major upgrade program called H-1.

The program calls for the corps' entire inventory of 180 Super Cobras to be rebuilt with a new four-bladed rotor system in place of the older two-bladed system. The addition of two more blades greatly increases the operational envelope of the Super Cobra. When fitted with the new four-blade rotor system, the UH-1W becomes the UH-1Z Super Cobra. The first Z versions of the Sea Cobra will enter operational use with the corps in 2004.

Another helicopter in service with the corps that carries an assortment of weapon systems is the UH-1N. A two-engine version of the army's famous UH-1 Huey helicopter, the UH-1N performs command and control functions, re-supply, and casualty evacuation for the marines. Weapons used as door guns on the helicopter include 7.62mm M240 and M2 .50-caliber machine guns. Launcher pods for 2.75-inch rockets may also attach to the exterior of the UH-1N if needed. When armed, the helicopter can provide suppressive fire in support of ground operations. Like the Sea Cobra, the corps' entire fleet of UH-1N helicopters will soon be rebuilt and upgraded, after which the helicopter will be assigned the designation UH-1Y.

Acronyms

AAAV	Advance Amphibious Assault Vehicle	**FASTs**	Fleet Antiterrorism Teams
AAK	Appliqué Armor Kit	**FAV**	Fast Attack Vehicle
AAV	Amphibious Assault Vehicle	**FEP**	Firepower Enhancement Program
ACE	Aviation Combat Element	**FFAR**	Folding Fin Aircraft Rockets
AFATDS	Artillery Tactical Data System	**FMF**	Fleet Marine Forces
AMC	Armored Motor Car Company	**GCE**	Ground Combat Element
AMRAAM	Advanced Medium Range Antiaircraft Missiles	**GDLS**	General Dynamics Land System Division
APDS-T	Armored-Piercing Discarding Sabot-Tracer	**GP**	General Purpose
AT/FB	Terrorism and Force Protection	**GPMG**	General-Purpose Machine Gun
ATACMS	Army Tactical Missile System	**HE**	High-Explosive
ATARS	Advanced Tactical Airborne Reconnaissance System	**HEAA**	High Explosive Anti-Armor
BAD	Blast-Attenuation Device	**HEI-T**	High-Explosive Incendiary Tracer
BAR	Browning Automatic Rife	**HIMARS**	High Mobility Artillery Rocket System
CBU	Cluster Bomb Unit	**HMG**	Heavy Machine Gun
CCIP	Continuously Computed Impact Point	**HMMWVs**	High Mobility Multipurpose Wheeled Vehicles
CE	Command Element	**HQMC**	Headquarters U.S. Marine Corps
CLU	Command Launch Unit	**HUD**	Heads Up Display
CQB	Close Quarter Battle	**IFAV**	Interim Fast Attack Vehicle
CQBW	Close Quarter Battle Weapon	**IFV**	Infantry-Fighting Vehicle
CSSE	Combat Service Supports Element	**IP**	Improved-Performance
DMR	Designated Marksman Rifle	**JDAM**	Joint Direct Attack Munitions
DU	Depleted Uranium	**JSF**	Joint Strike Fighter
DWFK	Deep Water Fording Kit	**JSOW**	Joint Standoff Weapon
EAAK	Enhanced Appliqué Armor Kit	**JSSAP**	Joint Service Small Arms Program Office
ECP	Engineering Change Program	**LAV-AD**	Air-Defense
EMD	Engineering and Manufacturing Development	**LAV-AT**	Antitank
EOD	Explosive Ordnance Disposal	**LAV-C2**	Command Vehicle
FAE	Fuel Air Explosive	**LAV-JLNBCRS**	Joint Light Nuclear-Biological-Chemical Reconnaissance Vehicle

LAV-L	Logistics Vehicle	**RDJTF**	Rapid-Deployment Joint Task Force
LAV-M	Mortar	**RIS**	Rail Interface System
LAV-MEWSS	Mobile Electronic-Warfare Support System	**RISE**	Reliability-Improved-Selected-Equipment Engine
LAV-R	Recovery Vehicle	**RTE**	Rifle Team Equipment
LAW	Light Antitank Weapon	**SACLOS**	Semiautomatic Command to Line-of-Sight
LGBs	Laser Guided Bombs		
LVA	Landing Vehicle Assault	**SASR**	Special Application Scoped Rifle
LVA5	Landing Vehicle Assault-Five	**SAW**	Squad Automatic Weapon
LVT	Landing Vehicle Tracked	**SLEP**	Service Life Extension Program
LVT1	Landing Vehicle Tracked-One	**SOC**	Special Operations Capable
LVT3	Landing Vehicle Tracked-Three	**SPMAGTF**	Special Purpose Marine Air-Ground Task Force
LVT7	Landing Vehicle Tracked-Seven		
MAGTF	Marine Air-Ground Task Forces	**SRAW**	Short-Range Assault Weapon
MCD	Missile Countermeasures Device	**STVOL**	Short Take Off and Vertical Landing
MEB	Marine Expeditionary Brigade	**TAD**	Towed Artillery Digitization
MEF	Marine Expeditionary Force	**TO&E**	Table of Organization
MEU	Marine Expeditionary Unit	**TOW**	Optically-Tracked Wire-Guided Missile System
MEU-SOC	Marine Expeditionary Unit Special Operations Capable		
		TUA	Under-Armor Turret
MICLIC	Mine-Clearing-Line-Charge	**TV/FLIR**	Television/Forward Looking Infrared Sight
MVTF	Military Vehicle Technology Foundation		
		UFH	Ultra-Lightweight Field Howitzer
MVTR	Medium Vehicle Tactical truck	**VB**	Vivien Bessier
MWS	Modular Weapon System	**VSEL**	Vickers Shipbuilding and Engineering Limited
NBC	Nuclear, Biological, Chemical		
Ops	Observation Posts	**VTOL**	Vertical Take Off and Landing
PLRS	Position Location Reporting System	**WSO**	Weapon System Operator
PWS	Precision Weapon Section		
RAM/RS	Reliability and Maintainability/Rebuild to Standards		
RAS	Rail Adapter System		

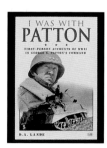
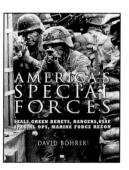